*The*
# DIARY
*of a*
# POLITICAL IDIOT

*The*

# DIARY

*of a*

# POLITICAL IDIOT

NORMAL LIFE IN BELGRADE

*Jasmina Tesanovic*

The publishers wish to thank the editors of *Granta*, where selections of the diary originally appeared, and especially Liz Jobey whose invaluable assistance made publication of this book possible.

Published in the United States by Midnight Editions, an imprint of Cleis Press Inc., P.O. Box 14697, San Francisco, California 94114.

Printed in the United States.
Cover design: Scott Idleman
Cover photographs: Jasmina Tesanovic—Stephanie Damoff
                              Belgrade—Hutchison Picture Library, London
Inside photographs: Stephanie Damoff
Text design: Karen Quigg
First Edition.
10 9 8 7 6 5 4 3 2 1

Tesanovic, Jasmina.
     Diary of a political idoit : normal life in Belgrade / Jasmina
Tesanovic.
        p. cm.
     ISBN 1-57344-114-7 (alk. paper)
     1. Tesanovic, Jasmina--Diaries. 2. Kosovo (Serbia)--History--
Civil War, 1998---Personal narratives, Serbian. 3.
Journalists--Yugoslavia--Belgrade (Serbia)--Diaries. 4. Bombing,
Aerial--Yugoslavia--Belgrade (Serbia) I. Title
     DR2087.7 .T47 2000
        949.7103--dc21
                                             00-047406

*Every book needs one ideal reader:*
*Stephanie Damoff was mine.*

# TABLE *of* CONTENTS

# NOTE FROM
# THE PUBLISHER

Hours after NATO started bombing Yugoslavia, Jasmina Tesanovic received an e-mail from a friend in Sweden, who wanted to know how she was doing. Jasmina didn't have time to write back, so she sent entries from her diary. Her friend, the writer Ana Valdes, posted Jasmina's diary entries on the web site of a magazine she wrote for. Within a week, the diaries had been posted anonymously on fifty web sites, translated into several languages and sent in emails throughout the world. Jasmina knew nothing of this. When a friend in London sent Jasmina an excerpt from the diary, she read a few paragraphs and thought, *This woman writes exactly like me.* Nevertheless, she did not believe she was reading her own diary until her friend traced the e-mail from Sweden to Holland to Croatia and back to Jasmina. Someone had removed Jasmina's name to protect her. The diary of an anonymous woman from Belgrade had become everybody's diary.

*The Diary of a Political Idiot* was chosen to represent the work of Serbian writers by the PEN Center. It was first published as a book in Argentina, thanks to another e-mail friend, Ana Ines Larre Borges, who translated the *Diary* into Spanish even as Jasmina was writing it. The *Diary* has now been translated into eleven languages. It first appeared in English in *Granta* (Issue 67).

A ruthless reviewer from Belgrade called *The Diary of a Political Idiot* "a book of the marginal for the marginal...the best book written this year, but it never will be mainstream in Serbia."

Midnight Editions was created to preserve just such "marginal" voices which, as Tim Judah writes, are often lost "because of the enormity of crimes committed in their names." Jasmina's *Diary* never made the news, the wire services, the major TV networks, or the mainstream magazines, but it has found its way into the hands of astute editors and readers around the globe. At a time when "compassion fatigue" is seen as both the cause and the unavoidable consequence of current international news reporting, we believe that Jasmina Tesanovic's wide readership is as much a testimony to the intelligence and compassion of her readers as it is to her own.

Frédérique Delacoste
San Francisco, August 2000

# INTRODUCTION

In June 1991 I was working for the London *Times* and the *Economist* as a foreign correspondent. I was based in Romania. One night, I received a call saying that since Slovenia, one of the six republics that made up the neighbouring Yugoslav federation, was on the brink of declaring independence, I should make my way there as quickly as possible to report on this event. Days later the shooting began.

Yugoslavia, forged during the Second World War by the communist leader Marshall Tito, a man whom Jasmina Tesanovic, and almost all of her generation had grown up thinking of as their benevolent grandfather, had begun its bloody descent into war.

I never went back to Romania, except to collect my family. The Slovene war lasted a bare ten days. Almost seamlessly, it rolled into the Croatian war. That summer I saw the first villages burn. Who would have believed that homes and villages would still be burning, in what is now the former Yugoslavia, almost ten years later?

In the months that followed I, like other correspondents, crept through the cornfields into Vukovar, the eastern Croatian town that was being besieged by the Yugoslav Army and various Serbian paramilitaries. Then I followed the Montenegrin soldiers as they burned and pillaged their way up to Dubrovnik. From within its great walls, we watched these soldiers pick off the boats in its little fishing port, while the population huddled for safety in its ancient towers.

And then came the cease-fire. Croatia, like Slovenia, had declared independence but unlike Slovenia had a substantial Serbian minority. Serbian leaders announced that if Croatia left Yugoslavia then Serbian areas of Croatia would leave Croatia. In this way, the short-lived Republic of Serbian Krajina, with its capital in the railway junction town of Knin, was born.

For a few months, as the United Nations deployed its "blue berets" in Krajina, it looked like the war might be over. After all, the doomsayers said that if there was a war in Bosnia, hundreds of thousands would die and whole cities would be destroyed. If nothing else, Bosnia's three nations—its Serbs, Croats, and Muslims—agreed on this. Just because they knew what would happen didn't stop it from happening however.

As the spring of 1992 broke, the Yugoslav Army began digging into siege positions around Sarajevo, the Bosnian capital. As in Croatia, Serbian leaders said that if

Bosnia were to leave Yugoslavia, Bosnia's Serbs would not join them. They would carve out their own state in Bosnia, which would then unite with mother Serbia. Soon the shells started falling on Sarajevo, while out in the countryside and in small towns, for the moment hidden away from the prying eyes of foreign journalists, the great waves of ethnic cleansing began. Hundreds of thousands of Muslims, and, in their turn, Croats and Serbs, too, were driven from their homes. To this day nobody knows how many died.

By the winter of 1992 the war had more or less settled down. Lines were drawn across the map of the old Yugoslavia, and now the Serbian flag flew from the border of Romania, across Serbia, across Bosnia and across Croatia, down to the azure waters of the Adriatic sea. For a brief moment it looked like the Serbs, led by Slobodan Milosevic in Serbia and Radovan Karadzic in Bosnia, had won. All Serbs lived in what they promised would become one state—Greater Serbia? A United States of Serbia? What did it matter what it was called, so long as the Serbs had won?

Then, in the summer of 1995, everything changed. Ratko Mladic, the Bosnian Serb military leader, took Srebrenica, an eastern Bosnian Muslim holdout. Revelling in victory, Mladic promised "revenge" on the "Turks" as he called them. Thousands of Muslim men and boys were rounded up or caught trying to flee and executed. To this day as many as 8,000 men are still unaccounted for.

Weeks later Croatian forces, with tacit U.S. approval, moved to reclaim the land they had lost to the Krajina Serbs. In three days they reconquered everything they had lost—and 170,000 Serbs fled in vast, pathetic columns. As they arrived in Serbia they were forced to dig in their pockets to pay their motorway tolls. There were now some 600,000 Serbian refugees in Serbia.

By November it was all over. The Bosnian Serbs, prodded by NATO air strikes, had agreed to peace talks at a U.S. Airforce base in Dayton, Ohio. Within weeks tens of thousands of NATO and other troops were pouring into Bosnia to enforce the peace.

But of course it wasn't over. In a very real sense, the cancer that destroyed the old Yugoslavia had begun in an obscure southern province of Serbia called Kosovo. Many predicted that it would end there as well.

The first lesson of the Balkans is to expect the unexpected. Many thought that if there were ever to be violence in Yugoslavia it would start in Kosovo, whose population was overwhelmingly ethnic Albanian and who had resented their incorporation into Serbia in 1912 and then into Yugoslavia in 1918 and, yet again, in 1944. But it did not happen this way. So now, all eyes turned to Serbia proper, physically unscathed by war, but led by Slobodan Milosevic, the man who was widely credited as having been the greatest single cause of conflict in the former Yugoslavia.

Throughout the last few years Serbia's mood had shifted. But, we must never forget, in a very real sense, the control wielded by Milosevic over most of the media was instrumental in manipulating his people. In 1992, as the Serbs went to war with Croatia, it seemed as if the only programs on television were documentaries about the wartime Croatian "Ustashas" and their murder of hundreds of thousands of Serbs in Croatia and Bosnia. "The Ustashas are back," trumpeted the television. "The Germans are after our ports on the Adriatic," ranted otherwise intelligent people, parroting this bizarrely old-fashioned propaganda line from TV Serbia.

During the conflict in Bosnia, Serbs were treated to the message that, in this "defensive" war, the Serbs were fighting the diabolical and combined forces of the Islamic-Vatican-Austro-Hungarian-revanchists. Diplomats complained that they wished Serbs had heads on their shoulders, not televisions, so hard was it to resist this propaganda. In many families the generation gap yawned into conflict. As Jasmina Tesanovic recounts, an older generation schooled in the ways of communist obedience now thought their own children traitors. Often this was not for having renounced communism but, in families like hers, for recoiling and sometimes denouncing the nationalism, or "fascism" as she says, that it had mutated into.

For her parents' generation it was hard to come to terms with the fact that either they had lived a lie, that the Yugoslav slogan of "Brotherhood and Unity" had never been more than rhetoric, or that a generation brought up to believe in their leaders now found it impossible to believe that their leaders were nothing more than cynical opportunists, interested in power and not in them, the people.

There were few who actively resisted the state's propaganda, but there were some, Jasmina included. There were brave groups organized around the magazine *Vreme*, the radio station B-92, the Women in Black protest group (to which Jasmina belonged), and a handful of other NGOs which either reported on what was really happening or tried to rally people against the war. The problem was that, in the latter task at least, they failed. To begin with, there was no mass feeling against the war, first because most Serbs were convinced, or rather had been convinced, that everything being done in their name, from Sarajevo to Srebrenica, was done to defend Serbs and second, because they were winning.

When the tide of war began to turn, when the war did not end, when life became tough in Serbia, this did not lead to protest against the war but to withdrawal. People no longer wanted to know what was happening in Croatia and Bosnia. What they did want to know was whether they would be paid this month, and how they would feed their families.

Hyperinflation took over from where inflation left off. Under tough international sanctions Serbia's black-marketeers flourished, and criminals flaunted their new-found wealth and moved to desirable residential streets like Jasmina's. By January 1994, the monthly inflation rate was 313,563,558 per cent. Expressed at an annualized rate, that was 851, 000, 000, 000, 000, 000, 000, 000, 000, 000, 000, 000, 000, 000, 000, 000, 000, 000, 000, 000, 000, 000, 000, 000, 000. Food, and everything else for that matter, simply disappeared from the shops. Who cared about Sarajevo, when you couldn't buy a loaf of bread in Belgrade? Not many.

In the end, hyperinflation was dealt with, and with the end of the war in Bosnia came hope. As Serbia began to return to normal, hundreds of thousands came out to protest against the theft of votes in local elections held in November 1996. For the first time, control of city halls in many towns and big cities, including Belgrade, had been won by the opposition. This was clear when votes were counted, but when the tallies were announced it appeared that Milosevic and his allies remained in control.

The protesters waved the Stars and Stripes and Britain's Union Jack. Europe and the West seemed to be their future. Every evening for eighty-eight days, they marched through the streets of Belgrade and other towns and cities. Eventually they won. The municipalities that the opposition had won in the contested election were handed over to them.

But Serbia's opposition did not prove up to the task of unseating Milosevic. The coalition, which had mobilized hundreds of thousands of mainly young and middle-class Serbs who wanted nothing less than the return of their future, collapsed. Its two main leaders, Vuk Draskovic and Zoran Djindjic, were no longer able to keep their animosities in check and they succumbed to Milosevic's skilful and successful strategy of divide and rule. On 15 July 1997, the triumphant Serbian president traded in his old job title for that of President of Yugoslavia, now consisting of just Serbia and the increasingly reluctant little Montenegro.

The collapse of the opposition was a crushing blow for ordinary Serbs. The war, sanctions and isolation had suspended ordinary life for six or seven years already. Ordinary middle-class Serbs, like Jasmina and her friends, had seen their incomes reduced to virtually nothing. People who used to travel abroad on holiday, just like other Europeans, suddenly found themselves walled in by a lack of visas and money, and now by a widespread antipathy to a people perceived as genocidal maniacs, rather than ordinary people trapped by a regime interested in power—and self preservation.

What was the way out? For most there was none. But hundreds of thousands, many of the best and the brightest, did leave. Thousands of young men left because they had no wish to fight in what they regarded as unjust wars. More left because they had no future in what had become Europe's pariah. Many of Serbia's best scientists, engineers and other professionals are in Toronto now, or London, or just scattered across the globe.

As Serbs considered their future, debated and argued, ever more people simply "tuned out" to the never-ending bad news about their country. They became, as Jasmina so rightly notes, indifferent. And this is why her diaries are so important. For the first time a western readership, who like Jasmina, is educated, liberal, and open-minded, can understand the mindset of a people caught in an appalling situation. It is easy for foreigners to judge; it is less than easy to say how *you* would react if you were a Serb.

In the years after Dayton, it was not just the Serbs who were considering their future. The Kosovo Albanians who, unwillingly, still shared a state with them, were now facing a radical choice. For years they had followed a policy of passive resistance. But it had come to nothing. Serbs consider Kosovo a sacred land, because of their medieval churches and monasteries there, but unlike in the middle ages, the vast majority of its population is now ethnic Albanian. They are a non-Slav people, who felt trapped inside the state of the south Slavs, which is what the word "Yugoslavia" means.

As it became clear that their policy of passive resistance had come to nothing, the hard men who said that the only way to achieve freedom was to take up the gun came to the fore. Slowly, but surely, a guerrilla war led by the Kosovo Liberation Army began. By the spring of 1998 it was escalating and, in their attempts to crush what was becoming a serious insurgency, the Serbian police chased hundreds of thousands into the hills. The West, fearful of another Srebrenica, was sucked in again.

Western leaders had been accused of indifference and political paralysis in dealing with Croatia and Bosnia. This time they moved to action, pushing for a diplomatically negotiated solution — despite a state-sponsored referendum in which Milosevic had invited Serbs to reject outside mediation. The offer was for an interim, three-year settlement, which would restore Kosovo's political autonomy but be enforced by a NATO-led peace keeping force as in Bosnia. Despite threats to bomb from NATO countries, intended to prod Milosevic into accepting the deal, he ultimately refused what many Serbs regarded as an offer designed to be rejected, but which diplomats believed was the last best chance for peace.

NATO began bombing Yugoslavia on 24 March 1999. With the experience of the Bosnian Serbs and Dayton behind them, western leaders believed that the action would last three days or, at most, a week. For his part, Milosevic believed that Russia would come to his aid and that NATO would fall apart. The bombing lasted a full 78 days until Milosevic capitulated.

Just as Jasmina did all she could to secure a visa to get out of the country, journalists like me did all we could to get in. Some, mostly those who had not reported on the wars in Croatia and Bosnia, succeeded. I, among others, was banned for those 78 days. Even if I had been allowed in, I could not have captured the "inside story" of how the war looked to ordinary Serbs, with whom most of us, I believe, can identify. It is this rare perspective that makes Jasmina's diaries unique and, for the historical record, so very valuable.

During those 78 days several hundred civilians, the figures vary, were killed by NATO bombs. At the same time, Serbian forces expelled, or caused to flee, 850,000 Kosovo Albanians and thousands, these numbers are also disputed, were killed. Some refugees were caught for days at Blace, in no-man's-land between Kosovo and Macedonia. Under the bombs few Serbs cared about the fate of the Albanians, indeed many thought that they deserved their fate. Jasmina and her circle of friends were honorable exceptions. Where possible they maintained contact with their Kosovo Albanian friends, and, in difficult circumstances, helped them when they could.

Voices of Serbian sanity, the voices of Serbs like Jasmina, people like you or me, are far too often lost because of the enormity of crimes committed in their name.

Crimes committed against Serbs can seem, especially to media editors, of little interest by comparison.

We in the West, not battered by endless mind-numbing propaganda, not under the stress of war or jaded and exhausted by years of isolation must not let ourselves fall prey to thinking that "they" deserve what they get. This is the importance of Jasmina's diary, because it shows us how "they" could be "us"; what it feels like, what it *is* like to be trapped in a country isolated by its regime, where completely ordinary people pay for the crimes of their leaders.

Tim Judah
London, August 2000

THE REPUBLICS OF THE FORMER YUGOSLAVIA

## THE FEDERAL REPUBLIC OF YUGOSLAVIA, 2000
(THE STATUS OF KOSOVO IS YET UNDETERMINED)

*The*
# DIARY
*of a*
# POLITICAL IDIOT

# PART ONE

*Prelude to War*

1998

**Jasmina Tesanovic**

Last night I was in a restaurant with a friend. It was dusk and we were sitting on the terrace overlooking the Danube when a swarm of mosquitoes attacked. There was pandemonium—women screaming and rushing inside, men moving chairs and tables out of their way. I thought if a single bomb landed here by mistake, their nationalism would vanish.

## 17 March

I tremble, my feet tremble while I am asleep. Why do my legs tremble as if an electric current is passing through them? Is it because I will need them to run away and fear they will fail me? I fear everything. I fear death and killing. I fear not being able to imagine the future. I watch my children with a sense of guilt. Here in Serbia in the eighties and nineties I should have been sensible enough to realize I should never have children.

When I was pregnant, in the eighties, we didn't have electricity for days. It was winter, and Tito had just died. Tito always told us we had lots of electricity. He said we were a rich country, the best in the world, and I believed him. I liked his face. I'd known it all my life. I thought he was my grandfather. Once, when I was a little girl and lived with my family in Cairo, I was supposed to give him flowers, but then they made me give flowers to President Nasser of Egypt instead, because I was taller and Tito was smaller, and Nasser was taller and the other girl was smaller. Since then I've always associated being small with privilege and beauty.

I grew up abroad, first in Egypt and then in Italy. My father was an engineer who became a businessman and my mother a pediatrician who gave up her career to follow him. I grew up switching between languages and cultures, going to an English school and speaking Serbian at home while the world around me spoke Arabic and then Italian. It was years before I managed to turn this painful Babylon in my head into an advantage, and now I am writing this diary in English, which for me is not the language of intimacy or love but an attempt at distance and sanity, a means of recalling normality.

## 20 March

It has been a terrible month. The killing has started again, this time in Kosovo. Once again we are witnesses who cannot see. We know it is going on, but we are blind. It's not even the killing that makes me die every day, little by little, it's the indifference to killing that makes me feel as if nothing matters in my life. I belong to a country, to a language, to a culture which doesn't give a damn for anybody else and for whom nobody gives a damn. And I am completely paralyzed. I am not used to fighting. I am not used to killing. I don't believe anybody anymore, not even myself. I have stayed here and I have made a mistake: victim or not, I have become one of those who did nothing for themselves or for those they love. I have a feeling that I will not survive.

## 22 March

Someone gave me some vitamins from California to make me stronger, but they made me feel drugged with useless, mindless energy. Is it possible that a whole nation can have been taking vitamins for years which made me crazy after only two days? They made me want to jump out of my skin. I went outside and marched round in the snow, and only then did I begin to feel myself again—weak and sick as before. Now I take only tea, chamomile, and a bit of decent food each day. Life still seems pointless, except for a few details. Sometimes somebody reads a book of mine and it makes them feel good. Then I feel useful—or at least not useless.

I spent yesterday evening with three young women who seemed so bright and happy—perhaps because their hopes are still intact. Even war and injustice can't completely destroy the hopes of those who haven't lived yet, like my daughter, who is only thirteen. They look up to me, these girls, they would like to be me in twenty years. They don't see my anxiety, my shattered inner self. They think I am wise and beautiful and sincere. And so I was—I was fine last night. We laughed about sanctions, about the war, about our destiny as people who will have to flee—because we know we will have to leave for a new life, otherwise we'll become like the others. My husband said every country has its terrible political and social upheavals, and some people run away from what they are born into. I know that's true, but here there is nowhere to run to except to places just as oppressive as those you are running away from. I know that despair from my first exile and I fear that choice.

In 1992, I was in Vienna, waiting for Belgrade to be bombed. I was a Serb in Austria, a country whose language I couldn't understand. Then in Italy it was even worse. I understood only too well that I was a bad Serb, guilty for not stopping the atrocities of war. And that made me more of a nationalist, as are most people who live in exile.

## 24 March

So what is normal life? I can't even wash the dishes without being philosophical about it. Is this the last time I'll be washing dishes? Will I have to spend the rest of my life washing dishes in exile?

## 25 March

Today they are talking about sanctions again. I don't bother to wonder what will become of us, I just know I have to survive. They say the mind never dies; well I think the mind dies first, if you are harassed enough. I am fighting to save my mind for a better time.

## 26 March

This is another politically-correct war rather than a moral one. I have seen it in Bosnia, in Croatia, and now in Serbia. Americans are being Americans and politically correct, which is painful for anyone who is not American and who is politically correct in a different way. Americans don't get it. We have a different idea of everyday life, we have different emotions, we have different thoughts about help. We perceive intrusive American help as helping the self-image of the American nation. In many ways we, both victims and aggressors, know that the Americans are right. We would all like to be Americans, but it's impossible. The Americans don't want us to be Americans, they want us to be the Other. They want us to be a territory where new plans can be implemented. I don't like feeling like this. Inside Serbia, I have taken the high moral position of a traitor. I defend foreigners, Americans, and foreign intervention against national barbarians. But I don't like to be thought of as the Other by anyone, particularly not the biggest power in the world.

The other night, my neighbors vandalized my car. They did it openly, saying they'd lost their cars, so why should I have mine? I know I should fight back, but how? The law doesn't exist anymore, and the police won't protect a woman with a luxury car. They believe only men should have luxury cars in Belgrade today.

My neighbor is a poor alcoholic who didn't adapt to the new ways of making money through crime, so he lost his money and his mind, and now he drinks beer all day on the pavement. He's neither a good man nor a bad man, just one of thousands of people who subsist in the moral and physical decay that is modern Serbia. He's not alienated from society. He is in touch emotionally and rationally. He understands the New Order and is following it. We are both part of the New Poor. Before last night, the only thing that divided us was my car parked on the pavement where he drinks his beer. So he tried to do away with the symbol that stood between us. I understand it. There's no point in explaining that cars shouldn't be scratched, or knifed, or spat upon. He has suffered, so why shouldn't my car? And the criminal on the other side of the street with the big red sports car watching us—it goes without saying—we know, he knows, everybody knows his car is not going to be touched because he carries a gun.

## 27 March

My parents are ashamed of me, ashamed of my choices. They suffer with every word I utter and rejoice at every word I don't. They want me silent and obedient. They say, "We gave you everything. Don't question it. Just keep this wonderful world we made going." The truth is, my generation won't have time to change much of anything. They are such brave parents, ready to sacrifice my life for their country. But I am a coward child, not ready to die for any country or to fight a war for any just cause. They and people like them fought all those Balkan wars, produced all these leaders who are ready to appeal to people to fight in more wars, for land, for graves, out of pride, out of prejudice. What I resent is that they never told me the truth about their lives. They never told me about their wars, or about how they survived hunger and killing to make their country perfect. Did they kill? Did they see people being killed? Was it all worthwhile?

## 7 April

Do we want to be ruled by foreigners or not? That's the question put to us in the upcoming referendum. Can it really be so simple? Here we have a ruthless dictator convincing us that we are the "Wild Serbs" we are not. He falsifies our thoughts, our roles, our desires, our history. We are drafted into a war we don't understand and don't want by cowards who are afraid to negotiate because they can't be rational.

I think of myself as a political idiot. Idiot, in ancient Greece, denoted a common person without access to knowledge and information—all women, by definition, and most men. I am unable to make judgements. I see no options I can identify with. Is that normal? Is it because I am a woman? The political options offered by my fellow countrymen sound aggressive, stupid or far-fetched when compared to my simple needs. I need to move, I need to communicate, I need to have children, I need to talk, I need to play, I need to have fun. They speak of historical rights and precedents, but it's not my history they speak of, or if it is, it's a history I had no part in. They talk of blood and of pride, but I am losing my mind because of a lack of love and understanding. All our instincts are focused on dying or surviving.

## 14 April

Yesterday, I jumped onto a bus, a terrible, stinking, falling-to-pieces bus. It was a dangerous trip from several points of view. The doors wouldn't close and people were hanging out of them, pick-pockets were everywhere, and several old, sick people who can't afford medicine were coughing and spitting on everybody. But riding on the bus, I realized I was surrounded by the happy, pretty faces of young schoolgirls. It was a group of ballet dancers coming back from a successful performance. I thought of their parents somewhere, gray and tired and anxious like me, young-old people gone half crazy with fear and worry. But watching these beaming faces, their arms and legs long and thin like some African tribe, I thought, my God, you can't stop beauty, you can't stop joy, you can't stop creativity. Their language was urban, but sharp and soft, as if they were from another century when women grew up secluded and educated in convents away from life and men. I looked through the window at downtown Belgrade, full of young boys and girls on a Saturday night, wearing the same shoes, the same jackets as kids in New York or Paris. Now I know some of them are criminals, and some of their parents starve in order to make them look like that. But even so, you can't stop joy and beauty. It grows faster than crime and death.

## 15 April

Today I saw a Serbian family in the street in front of the UNHCR [United Nations High Commissioner for Refugees] office near my flat in the center of the city. Their bags and suitcases blocked the sidewalk. They were terrified. The middle-aged woman was crying, her young girl was ashamed to meet our gaze, and the men just sat and stared at the pavement in front of them. Men often do that when they become powerless. It made me shiver. They were in my city, on my street, Serbian refugees from Kosovo. And we shared a common destiny.

Some twenty years ago my aunt had to emigrate from Kosovo with all her family because, as Serbs, they were harassed by the Albanians. They left all their belongings, sold their house at a loss, and started life anew here on the outskirts of Belgrade. That is a common experience in my father's family. They came from Herzegovina and are now scattered all over the world.

The family in the street reminded me of other families I have seen in the past years, though at that time only a few came to Belgrade. This time all the Kosovo Serbs will come here. My city will change once more. But then I doubt it is really mine. I don't feel safe here, or happy, or free. I'm a refugee in my own city.

My mother, as a communist, refused to acknowledge the life of her father, whom she considered a kulak. I refuse the culture of my mother, whom I consider a fanatic.

My child is burning bridges with me because I am a traitor and she believes in national values. There is no continuity except in the rejection of the values that went before. An old lady I know burned her own library, before the Second World War, because she was a communist and her family library had been built with "dirty" money. She burned the whole house—her father's house—by mistake. And she never felt sorry. The only tradition is that of rejection and breaking with the past. Even small family objects are thrown away, valuable or not, in order to erase, to forget, to make a free space for the future. But is it possible to live on such shifting, tumultuous ground?

## 16 April

Sanctions are nearly certain. Some people are saying, well, we had sanctions before, in 1992 and then again in 1993—at least we know what we're in for. But others say they just can't go through it all again.

## 18 April

Tomorrow is Orthodox Easter. Everybody is celebrating something they never used to do. They are faking religion. How long can one fake something that belongs to the inner core of one's life? I want to shout at my sick mother who invokes communism and war as she bakes traditional food. I want to shout when she talks about Kosovo in front of my innocent child who doesn't want to know anything about history or politics because she can't stand to know anyone is suffering. My daughter puts her hands over her ears, remembering the family fights over nationalism when she was small and we argued continuously whether we should leave the country or not.

But I can't speak because I, too, am faking normality, pretending that we lead a normal, everyday life based on good old-fashioned values of friendship, loyalty and sisterhood. But when I walk down the street and look in the eyes of someone from whom I might expect understanding, I see the eyes of a maniac looking back at me. Doctors look like their patients. We suffer the same disease of loss of nerves, tolerance and faith. Our humanity is reduced to base existence.

The pensioners are being told they have to vote "yes" in the referendum in order to get their pensions and be able to buy bread or anything else. The result of our referendum is already pretty certain. Nobody dares to challenge Big Brother and his political murals on which our personal lives are splattered like cheap paint.

## 20 April

This morning I couldn't buy milk. Just as six years ago, when the war started, it started with milk, a symbol of maternal need. The message is: death to the children.

## 21 April

A few years ago, a corpse was found chopped up in pieces in my dustbin on Molerova Street. It was discovered by the gypsy drunkard who lives in the basement of my building with his crippled wife, five cats and two dogs. The cats and dogs sleep on the bed, the drunk and his wife sleep on the earthen floor, and they all live on scraps which they scavenge by rummaging through the garbage bins. The murder was a very famous case. A sixteen-year-old boy had killed his best friend because of a small unpaid debt. He hid the corpse in the cellar for a few years, then in the attic, and finally, when the corpse started to smell too badly, he threw the decaying bits into the bin around the corner. My street, my bin. This sixteen-year-old killer lived in a beautiful building with fancy windows that I had noticed were always open. He was airing out the corpse. I thought his open window was some kind of protest against the war, because during the demonstrations in 1997, people would protest from their open windows with flashing lights, music, or noise.

My street, Molerova Street, is famous. Until a few years ago, the red bourgeoisie lived here. Then, when the war in the former Yugoslavia began anew, rich people moved in; theirs was dirty money, if not bloody. Now my street is lined with expensive cars, fancy cafés, shops, and some very strange people with shaved heads and guns. They took over the beautiful flats by paying off the bourgeoisie who by then were very poor—though I can't feel too sentimental about that. Yesterday, a gypsy band passed through our street and the criminals in their cars slowed down, respecting the old Belgrade tradition. But normally, if you take one of their parking places, they'll take away your car and you'll never see it again. The police work with them, it's obvious.

## 24 April

The referendum was yesterday. One of my friends said, now they'll come and shoot us because we didn't vote. I told her she was just being paranoid. After the vote, our president gave a speech. Everything about him, his face, his voice, his words, and his emotions, was so familiar— that pathetic, patronizing tone that says he knows what's best for me, just like my father. This president, whom I know to be a corrupt liar and merciless enemy, worries for my future—that is why he is sending me to war, that is why he is fighting the rest of the world. That is why he makes me weep.

## 30 April

We spent yesterday evening with an American friend. She was asking us how we could still talk to friends who had become nationalists. I was so nervous I could hardly sit down. Then we heard the news. We've got sanctions. Our friend was afraid her plane wouldn't leave. She asked me what the sanctions were about, what our lives would be like. I said, I don't know. I can't control my life anymore. I feel utterly depressed, absolutely lonely.

At the beginning of the Serbo-Croatian war, we went to the International PEN Congress party in Vienna. Nobody wanted to sit at a table with me and my husband—with Serbs—but an Austrian writer came with his wife to our table and talked to us without mentioning the war. I thought we were safe in our invisible pain. But at the end of the evening, he simply said, "If you need money, if you need a flat, any time, we are here."

I started crying, and he said, "I remember when I was eleven, I was a Nazi for five minutes." His name was Peter Ebner and his father was killed as a German soldier at the Russian front.

**6 May**

Today I went to a meeting of the Women in Black. We were about fifty women—feminists, refugees, activists, women running nongovernmental organizations (NGOs), women driven mad by the past wars—plus a few gay men. Most of the women from NGOs and feminist groups saw a parallel in Kosovo to the past wars in Croatia and Bosnia. I saw it differently. We have had an apartheid state for Albanians in Serbia for the past ten years at least. In Croatia and Bosnia, it wasn't like that. That was about boys' games and loot.

I was so upset I could hardly speak. "The police are entering houses to mobilize men all over Serbia..." Some of the women suggested peace caravans, peace protests, pacifist walks, and a global protest against mobilization. But we did all that six years ago and nobody listened to us, so why would they listen now?

## 9 May

Today the international community decided on another package of sanctions against Yugoslavia. One more step on the path to total isolation. I was in the marketplace where people were talking about prices and inflation, but the hole in the middle of their sentences represented their knowledge of what had happened. Today the president's wife opened a maternity hospital in Novi Sad. For two hours everything came to a standstill. Women already in labor were sent away. But no political power in the world can prevent children from being born. Only afterwards can power transform a precious little life into a miserable existence without a future. Yes, power can do that.

## 16 May

What are they doing to us? We are entering the long tunnel of fascism, fascism with a domestic face, that of your neighbor who beats his wife when she disobeys, and pisses on the staircase when drunk. The face of a funny big man who is dangerous because he doesn't know his or your boundaries.

## 26 May

I went to the Montenegro coast, to a village. Three men were sitting on the steps and drinking beer from the bottle. They were workers building houses in this small village without people and with only a few houses. They were watching a small dog on the pavement left by his bitch mother, then staring at different points on the horizon, and one of them was telling a tale. He was a philosopher as well as a storyteller, a Homer. He said: there is no use in being too intelligent, too rich, too smart, too ambitious. . . That is not what life is all about. And all this money and politics and power, who cares, only fools. Because I know better. Listen to this true story: "There was a man who left his home, wife and children to buy cigarettes round the corner. Once in the street he entered a crack in time. He was snatched by a hole in space in time. He didn't realize that: he bought his cigarettes and went back straight home. For him, only five minutes had gone by, but in the meantime twenty years had passed for his wife and children. His wife was dead, his children old. And he was still the same, unaware of what had happened. Now, that is what life is all about: the only sense you can make out of it is to put a stone over a stone, every day, build a house, love a dog, kiss a woman, pat a child. Then you drink your beer sitting on the steps of your unbuilt house, waiting for your unborn children and knowing of the crack in time. That is what life is all about."

Today the nationalists passed a new law against the autonomy of the university. They say students should just study and not care about politics. Those who protested were beaten and some of them were arrested. Everybody else was confused and silent. Most people here have been completely broken down by the political shit of the past five—the past fifty—years. Maybe there will be strikes, protests, but more likely nothing will happen at all, and we'll be back in the dark ages. Does anybody enjoy this parade of totalitarianism? Are these few in power good for anyone? I don't believe so. Serbs are like women who don't want to be feminists; they're satisfied with the old stereotypes, no equality, just invisibility. I can see how that happens. I used to feel that way, too. It's a natural state, you're born into it. Once you come out of it, you may lose everything, but there is no going back.

## 29 May

I met some people from the university. There will be no mass protest against the totalitarian laws. My friend who teaches at the university and whose father is a retired professor said he told her triumphantly, "Now you'll have to obey. Now you'll have no more freedom." This is a war between us and our parents, between political idiots (like me) and political criminals (like them)—no winners, no losers, no right ways, no middle ways, only permanent struggle and bad dreams.

### 3 June

A few days ago, a young soldier was killed during his regular training on the Kosovan border with Albania. Yesterday, his last letter to his parents was published in the paper. He couldn't have written anything more direct, cruel and true, "Just stop it, all of you who think you are doing something right, just stop it." I could imagine what his parents felt. I could have been his mother.

Some years ago, I found myself in the lift in my building with the mother of my next-door neighbor, a soldier who had been killed at nineteen. He was a punk, he wore an earring, and he played loud music. But when I saw her I started crying. I didn't know what to say. She embraced me and kissed me on both cheeks.

"Now, now, stop it, he was a brave boy and he died for his country," she said.

I wanted to shout at her, "You're crazy, you know it's not true, he was killed by people who were taking everything from us, our lives, values, goods, children." But then I saw her face. I knew she knew it. But she knew better, too. She was pleading with me silently: don't say it, don't take his death away from me. Death took him, leave me his death to be my company through life. (Mothers, I thought, traitors to the nation, traitors to their men, bearers of life and death, but never able to decide it. Mothers are like court jesters. They tell the truth but it has no impact.) She closed the lift door after me. His music will never disturb me again. Very soon I moved out. The silence was too much like my inner solitude. I couldn't bear it.

## 4 June

The cheapest photocopying shop in town is on my street. To reach it, you have to climb a narrow staircase over the cellar where the gypsies live. They're an institution in my street. In the last few years, the son has fathered two babies and now they are seven in one room. They all drink and make scenes, swearing, cursing and making fun of passers by. It was one of them who found the famous body in the dustbin. Today I went to the store to photocopy my stories for some Swiss friends. Coming out, I found the old gypsy woman lying in a pool of blood. She was screaming at her husband, "Radovan, you are killing me." He was running round her, and their dog was licking her blood. The babies were a few feet away, but not crying. I stepped over the blood and decided to leave them to it. Other people were doing the same. She lay there screaming for another half an hour until her husband pulled her to her feet and cleaned her up. They were both so drunk they could hardly stand. Then they sat on their usual doorstep and opened another bottle of beer. The babies didn't cry, the dog didn't bark. We're used to their love quarrels. Usually she beats him and he rarely strikes back, since he's smaller and less aggressive. She has a big handsome lover who comes over sometimes when the husband is away, and when he comes back, they all scream and fight, usually all night. We can't sleep because of the noise, but their quarrels are so interesting we just stand at the window and listen.

### 7 June

A friend of mine, a translator accompanying a journalist to Kosovo, was so moved by what she saw down there, she came back transformed. She's usually very arrogant, but as she explained how the Albanians were illiterate, frightened, and manipulated by their own leaders, not only persecuted by the Serbs, arrogance fell away. I know she's telling the truth. I remember how the girls from villages in Kosovo who came to feminist meetings in Belgrade had to pass through checkpoints and terror four times on every visit: first from their own people, for communicating with us Serbs; then from the Serbian police for leaving their home territory; then on the way back they were beaten, questioned, and insulted by Serbian police, for the same reason; and finally they were suspected by their relatives and friends of being traitors. Some of them were in traditional Muslim dress, others were in jeans, like women elsewhere in Yugoslavia. But their journey was through time as well as space. They had to be careful not to fall through the crack in time and be swallowed up.

I hear many policemen have refused to fight in Kosovo—hundreds of them—and they are losing their jobs but retaining their pride and honor. I am relieved; they are saving my pride and honor, too. For once I feel I am not, after all, living among wild men and savages, among killers and idiots. Maybe, after all, this is a place like any other, a place where policemen with good pay give up their jobs for moral reasons. Any reasons are welcome, as long as they give up fighting. Civil disobedience is the only thing that we have left to fight with.

## 8 June

All over Belgrade men huddle together in bars, whispering about the future over their beers. They say blood will flow on the streets of Belgrade in two weeks. They say we will all die of hunger, disease, and street violence. They say our country is finished, our children are doomed, we have no future. I have listened very carefully to these men who both move me and depress me. But I don't believe their stories. They're like little boys, these men, afraid to be killed but ashamed to cry. They'd rather damn the world than to say no to the war.

## 10 June

Last night, at 4:00 A.M., right under my window, a notorious criminal who lives a few doors away from me killed a young guy because he was in a car with the criminal's ex-girlfriend. The ex-girlfriend lives on my street, too, and I recognize her when she passes by. It was cold-blooded murder. The girl was screaming, "Don't kill him, he has nothing to do with me, he is a friend of my friend taking me home…" And still my neighbor fired five bullets into the guy's head. We heard it all, we saw his brain all over the car, all over the street. I went back to sleep. I couldn't feel anything except exhaustion. It is the fourth murder on my street in three years, not counting the two bombs in a restaurant.

My gypsy neighbor bit her husband so he slashed her with a bottle. Today, she was walking naked on the street. She said she felt natural and pretty. She reminded me of the artist Kulik, who, at a performance in Zurich some years ago, chained himself up as a dog, naked, and bit his audience. He said he wanted to show the death of civilization, the death of art. He said, "Art is dead, only artists are left behind." He claims we are in a prehuman rather than a posthuman stage. He believes this decaying of society makes way for new life. He has been arrested more than once in big Western cities during his performances.

## 12 June

We are expecting NATO troops to bomb selected targets in Kosovo and in Yugoslavia. It might end the war there — I wish it would — or just result in all-out war. Everybody is speculating, but I'm over the war shivers now. I had them so strongly six years ago when I left for Vienna that the thought of them now seems no more than an echo. Fear, like pain, has a natural limit. After that comes indifference.

### 17 June

Parents from all over the country are protesting against their children being sent to fight in Kosovo. I wish I could see their faces. They must be special people to admit that this is the same old war they once backed and that has been going on for the past sixty years.

### 18 June

The woman who helps me with my housework is a refugee from Knin, Croatia. During the Storm operation of 1995, they were bombed at five in the morning and fled in nightgowns, on foot or on tractors. She is trembling, can't sleep and is afraid it will happen again here. She wants me to calm her down but I feel exactly as she does. I tremble, too; I don't sleep, either. We both feel guilty for being in the wrong place once again, for having children we can't protect. And our men blame us for the same things. I tried to explain to her that it is not our fault, that our feelings of responsibility and guilt are irrational. But they are as real as they are ridiculous and groundless. Our fear and anxiety is so enormous that we clean, dust, and cook all day long, only interrupting the housework to listen to the news. We behave exactly the same, my cleaning woman and I. In Vienna, six years ago, I behaved exactly like my Bosnian refugee friends whose houses were bombed while mine was still standing. We go on cleaning and feel guilty.

## 20 June

I saw the children off—they're taking the bus to Greece. I'm staying to wait for NATO. People are betting whether NATO will bomb Belgrade now or at the beginning of September. They're not upset. Their minds are on tomorrow's football match between Yugoslavia and Germany. This makes the old communists angry. Bombing is a serious matter, they say.

I dropped by the women's center. A friend asks if I've heard what the policemen are doing in Kosovo. We continuously receive e-mails, she says. They rape, they kill, the same as in 1992 in Bosnia. On television we only hear about the Serbian people's centuries of suffering. An American woman asks me if I want to go to Kosovo and see for myself. But I don't have to. I can imagine how it is.

## 23 June

Tension in the air like electricity before a storm. The gypsy woman in the basement is lying half naked on the pavement, covered in spit, rolling on the glass from her broken beer bottle. Not even the conceptual artist Marina Abramovic in her latest performances could be that good. She's drenched in blood. "Police! Help me!" she shouts.

"They tried to kill me." Then she gives us a long speech about life, love, war and simplicity. She does this more and more frequently. Every day, I feel as though the social and emotional space between her and me is becoming smaller. When she sees me she says "Hello sweetie."

**5 July**

Last night, in front of a police station in the center of Belgrade, I saw a dozen policemen with sleeping bags and machine guns ready to leave for Kosovo. Their families were with them, mothers, fathers, wives, babies. The policemen were young and completely calm; the families were worried. It was unnerving to have to pick my way through the guns and sleeping bags on the pavement. I didn't dare ask them anything, not even to look after their machine guns so we could cross the street safely. They behaved as if their guns owned the sidewalk. In my country uniforms always take away the power of speech from citizens because uniforms carry guns, and citizens carry fear. So there is a permanent civil war going on between uniforms and civilians.

The Serbian alleged war criminal who destroyed a city in the war with Croatia, killing many people, committed suicide in the Hague. His body was brought back to Serbia for burial. People are talking about him as if he were a hero.

## 7 July

Today is a state holiday, something to do with the Second World War. The shops are closed. Old people haven't had their pensions delivered for a month, and even then they only received half the miserable sum. The black market is full of people who have dragged themselves through the humid heat to get a carrot, an onion, a tomato for free. The gypsy woman under my window is singing her lungs out in a lullaby to a baby who cannot sleep because of her song. It's like a scene from a cabaret. I feel sick, I can't breathe because of all the dirt and sadness. Everything is falling apart, no pensions, no cash on the streets, and in the shops, no sugar or oil. Foreigners are deciding our fate, without much knowledge or goodwill, but with energy and anger. Wild Serbs make the world go wild, they say. I wonder if we will have public soup kitchens in a few months' time and coupons for buying clothing, as my parents did after the Second World War. Normality is a myth by now.

## 12 July

Last night I was in a restaurant with a friend. It was dusk and we were sitting on the terrace overlooking the Danube when a swarm of mosquitoes attacked. There was pande- monium—women screaming and rushing inside, men moving chairs and tables out of their way. I thought if a single bomb landed here by mistake, their nationalism would vanish. Their proud Serbian nationalist small talk would fizzle out like air from a balloon. My friend and I stayed outside. The mosquitoes drowned in our sauce, and we ate it and them as they ate us. The nationalists left all their food behind on the terrace as if it were free. It reminded me of those stories about the Russian aristocracy during the October Revolution, but a cheaper version.

## July 18

Is there such a thing as happiness? Yes, there is. I remember being happy, maybe for seconds, but I remember clear images of bright states of mind and spirit. And that sense of coziness in the cold world...

These days in Serbia, the fascist government is turning the universities into primitive schools of concrete knowledge where creativity is banned and individual enterprise dangerous. Everywhere you turn, people are talking obsessively. Money, the weather, survival; there is no music, no joy. I avoid people.

## 31 August

Today a wonderful light fell on Belgrade. I nearly said to my husband, "I love you, let's have another child and stay here forever." Otherwise, I'm packing in my head, switching through countries like satellite channels: who would accept me? Hardly anybody, but still, the more countries I exclude, the closer I get to the one waiting for me.

## 30 September

My cousin has been hospitalized for AIDS. She is dying. She got better, and then she got worse. I went to see her when we had an earthquake. Everybody was out on the streets thinking it was NATO bombs. But she escaped the earthquake, and she would escape the bombs. She looked like a saint, a beautiful medieval picture, small, white and immobile. She smiled at me, and I didn't dare cry. I just wanted to faint. Who cares about bombs or earthquakes if you have even a chance to stay alive? She has none. With her will go my childhood, my ideals, my dreams. Who cares about NATO if she is gone? I don't want to be left alone with the dreams of happiness, beauty and bliss we shared as children.

During the night I hold my child tightly, trying to repair the bliss of childhood, but it is no use. There is no bliss in it. I see my dying cousin every day. I feed her as when we were kids. I say, stay alive. She says, I have no place to go. I say, stay alive for me, I will find you a place. Her eyes sparkle, she takes hold of my hand feebly. She still has beautiful hands. I say, promise.

In the hospital ward the water tubs are full of vomit. Most of the expensive medicines are unavailable and food is brought in from outside. The patients share their food. People don't stay long in the AIDS department. Relatives rush in and out, out of duty and fear. The nurses don't talk to patients or visitors. They think they already know everything—those who cross this threshold, abandon all hope. But then all hospitals here have had this kind of atmosphere for the past five or six years. Death reigns.

My father spent hours waiting for the hospital to open in order to be among the first to get a pacemaker. It wasn't a question of money, but of sanctions: no pacemakers for Serbs. And he got it. When he had a heart attack, there was no money for batteries for the machine to regulate his heart. Then the young man in the next bed died. I happened to be there. My father said, "The poor man, he died, grab his covers, I have none." And I did, I grabbed the covers from this dead stranger while his body was still warm. And as I did it, I felt a connection to him. Through his warm covers he had suddenly become familiar to me. I thought, this is not death, this is murder. And I got angry. Let's find the murderer.

## 10 October

Yesterday, in the queue to pay new taxes—for the war to come, for the monasteries, for weapons against Kosovar Albanians, for refugees, for NATO, for the whole world— I saw that people were worse off than I ever realized. They were rude and dirty and untidy, and when I looked at my image in the mirror, my hair was dirty, too. As a protest, I am not washing my hair.

These people despise people like me who are afraid, even if I'm their own flesh and blood. For some incredible reason they believe that bombs are part of everyday life. They clean their cellars, buy their candles, and say they will defend their country until the very end. Is it possible nobody is afraid? Is it possible that pride can win over fear, and if so, where is *my* pride? I am not proud of my proud people who have killed and humiliated others. Even if they did it under orders, they still did it. And yet I am not ashamed of my people, because I don't consider them any worse than most others; as such, I just see them as people who haven't had a chance to be better.

Yesterday night, I went with the Women in Black to demonstrate in the Square of the Republic. The police protected us from the crowd who were spitting on us and shouting, "Whores, Whores..." We'd all taken small rucksacks with ID, money, spare clothes, etc., in case we got arrested and tied to the trees as NATO targets—which is what Seselj, the vice-president of the Serbian government, promised us traitors. My parents call me a traitor for not supporting them; my husband does the same for not supporting him, my daughter, too.

### 11 October
Can anything be as bad as this feeling that imminent death is a lottery? Last night we had a birthday party. We couldn't get drunk, yet we couldn't stop laughing. It was the kind of behavior I've observed at funerals.

## 13 October

Is our fear great enough to make up for all the pain the Serbian people have caused to others since 1991? I can't say I would give my life for any cause. I'm not a hero. On the contrary, I am one of my country's few explicit, outspoken cowards. But I would give my life to avoid feeling this fear again, to avoid preparing bomb shelters. This time, instead of buying cans of food and bottles of water, I thought about buying pills for temporary and even permanent sleep—in case I lose my strength to survive or want to keep my children from realizing how senseless and unjust life can be.

## 15 October

Today is the demonstration against the banning of two independent newspapers. I am not sure many people will come. People are in shock, flattened under the heavy propaganda of what is good or bad for them. Mainly they are silent, afraid to think, afraid to pronounce judgements. Their lives are changing too fast. They're living on the edge.

## 18 October

Last night, the night of the new NATO ultimatum, I wanted to die. Just like my gypsy friend, I got drunk, drugged and aggressive. I wanted to kill. I bashed my head and concussed myself, made my nose bleed, and ended up with a broken finger. I wanted to excise the conflict inside me—the conflict all around me. *There. My war.*

## 13 November

My cousin died on November 10th. I had a vision two days before that it would happen, the day, the hour. I went to the hospital. They wouldn't let me in, so I stood in front of her window when she died. It was a beautiful day, sunny and clear. I entered the ward, gave the flowers I had brought to a very thin guy who seemed nice and very sick. The young lady doctor didn't mention the word AIDS when I asked the immediate cause of death. She said, "You know what this ward is for." This is exactly how all people involved with AIDS—whether patients or doctors or relatives—deal with it, through evasion. When I left the hospital I went for a long walk. I felt privileged to have been there, for having such a lovely cousin who made even a ghostly sickness like AIDS lovely. She was calm, smiling, and at peace. She even confessed her sins to the Head of the Serbian Church when he came to visit the ward, though she wasn't religious and I doubt she thought she had committed any sins, even if her life, seen from the outside, was a sin. My lovely cousin was a junkie, an outcast, and a writer who never published because telling her story would have meant losing her friends, her social security, and her job.

# PART TWO

*NATO*

1999

## Mica

My old friend Mica, the gypsy woman from the basement, has been rather stable since the bombings started. The difference between us, a white girl and a gypsy girl, is marginal now. We both live in basements with too many emotions, too few cigarettes, and too much beer.

**On January 15, 1999, Serb Interior Ministry troops invade the village of Racak in Kosovo and murder forty-five people.**

## 19 January

*My mother.* I wash her, soaping and rinsing the body that carried me for nine months. Her body is small and withered, yet her mind is completely alive, aggressive and dangerous. She hates me, she adores me. She wants to say goodbye to me, but she dares not, she says. Her body smells. She has been lying for weeks, immobile. Her hair is like baby's hair, and I am combing it, cutting her nails, crying, and holding back vomit in my throat. She mutters to herself. She can't stand the humiliation of being washed by me. My father looks away. We all wish you well, he says. Will I end this way too? At least my daughter has not been brought up to take care of me; somebody else will wash my body.

It is snowing outside, and the city is gray, dirty, and chaotic—Belgrade under sanctions, facing bombs, facing civil war. My mother says Clinton is a dirty old man—his women will get him in the end. I think, Milosevic is a dirty old man, but I say nothing. It is her hospital, it is her operation. All her worse character traits are coming out: her lack of tolerance, her bad hygiene, her anxiety, her lack of courage or optimism. She smiles at me, meaning, you know nothing about life—but unfortunately

I do. I have inherited her fear and I hate her for that. When her decayed body is taken down to the operating room, my father and I leave the hospital. We wait for a taxi, and he speaks of how lonely he will be without my mother. I say, she is not only your wife; she is my mother. Let's not speak about her as if she were dead. Let's not speak at all.

Later, I walk down the dirty streets talking to myself: I wish I were pregnant, who knows why...

## On 24 March, 1999, NATO begins air strikes against Yugoslavia.

### 26 March , 5:00 p.m.

I hope we all survive this war: the Serbs, the Albanians, the bad guys and the good guys, those who took up arms, and those who deserted, the Kosovo refugees traveling through the woods and the Belgrade refugees traveling the streets with their children in their arms looking for nonexistent shelters as the sirens go off. I hope NATO pilots don't leave behind the wives and children I saw crying on CNN as their husbands took off for military targets in Serbia. I hope we all survive, but that the world as it is does not: the world in which a USA congressman estimates twenty thousand civilian deaths as a low price for peace in Kosovo, or in which President Clinton says he wants a Europe safe for American schoolgirls. When Milosevic says we will fight to the very last drop of blood, I always feel they are talking about my blood, not his.

The green and black markets in my neighborhood have adapted to the new conditions: no bread from the state but a lot of grain on the market; no information from state TV, but a lot of talk among the frightened population about who is winning. Teenagers are betting on corners as if this was a football match. Whose planes have been shot down, ours or theirs? Who is the best liar? Who takes the most victims? Who wins the biggest victories?

The city is silent but still working. Rubbish is taken away, we have water, we have electricity, but where are the people? Everybody is huddled together, waiting for the bombs, people who hardly know each other, people who pretended not to or truly didn't know what was going on in Kosovo, people who didn't believe NATO was serious all along. We all sit together and share what we have. A feminist friend asked me to organize a conscious-ness-raising group. Another wants me to go with her to Pancevo, the bombed district on the other side of Belgrade, to give a reading of my novel. But there is no petrol. We'll have to buy bicycles.

The children phone each other all the time, pass-ing information back and forth. They prefer to be doing something in an emergency. We grown-ups nag at them with our fears, but they're too young for speculation.

They deal with facts and news. Most of them are informed through the children's networks, foreign satellite stations, and local TV.

I think of our Albanian friends in Kosovo. They must be much worse off than we are, and fear springs up at the thought.

I'm sleeping heavily, without dreams, afraid to wake up, but happy there is no real tragedy yet; we're all still alive, looking at each other every second for proof. And yes, the weather is beautiful. We enjoy it and fear it: the better the weather, the heavier the bombing; yet the better the weather, the more precise the bombing. I only wish I knew if we needed bad weather or good weather to stay alive.

The sirens are interrupting me, a terrible wailing up and down. I switch on CNN to see why sirens are going off in Belgrade but they don't know. Local TV will tell us when it's all over.

### NATO steps up air strikes against Yugoslavia.

**28 March**
Belgrade is rocking, shaking, trembling. We are entering the second phase of NATO intervention. The sirens went off today for nearly twenty-four hours. I had to go out to

buy some food, though we are not really starving yet, at least not keeling over. People are either taking tranquilizers or crying. The shelters are crowded. Every evening we go to the shelter in my local underground station. I know people there. We try to make plans and watch the news, none of it good, none of it reliable. The gypsies and the adolescents are the most frightened. The gypsies have been persecuted for centuries; the adolescents want their lives back.

I watch Jamie Shea at the NATO press conference. He makes what's happening to us here sound unimportant compared to NATO's aims. But how can anything be as simple as he makes it sound? If it were that simple, he would be God—and I don't think I could stand a military God any better than a religious one.

We've heard from our friends in Kosovo. They are already living through what will probably come to us in a few days, killing, looting of flats and houses, complete anarchy. For the time being most of us are staying underground. Somebody said that there are eight million Serbs underground, though I think it's part of the local propaganda, to keep people from coming out and making trouble. It's the opposite of the demonstrations of 1997 when everybody was out on the streets. Maybe we should set up an underground state with new democratic laws. Maybe this time it should be run by women and children.

People sheltering in the station have been living inside the trains for days. At first they were restless, hanging round the platforms and on the escalators. Now they barely have room to sit down and the air is stale. Some of my friends, a family of refugees from Krajina with two grown-up sons, spent five years under much worse conditions, so to them this is nothing. To me, it looks like a trans-Siberian journey to nowhere, but I visit them regularly, bringing them food and blankets. They can't understand why I go outside. I tell them of course I'm afraid, but I'm even more afraid of obediently staying underground for the next twenty years.

### 29 March

Gloomy, raining, the siren going all the time. I've just heard that martial law has been declared, with execution as punishment. I still can't believe we're living in war. In a few hours my life has changed completely, everybody's has. I think we're all becoming different people.

### 30 March

Today no bombs, no sirens to wake me up. I slept for sixteen hours. Last night the children went to a terrible nationalist rock and folk concert for people living underground. Afterwards I heard a gang of nationalists destroyed McDonald's.

My father used to dream of bombing long after the Second World War ended. He would wake up during the night, take me out of my bed, and carry me down to the basement. I remember him doing it, and last night I did it myself, carrying my daughter to safety several times. I feel sick both emotionally and physically. I feel like sleeping and sleeping forever—or until peace returns.

My God, we really are at war. I just heard some of the rules: no contact with the foreign press, court martial for deserters. Mental patients have been turned out on the streets, and the hospital beds are being saved for the wounded. My women friends are all working in various humanitarian centers with refugees, gypsies, and old, frightened women who live alone. My best friend says it's the only way she can stay sane. I'm different, the only way I can get rid of my emotions is by writing. I have to fight for my computer. It's the only one at home and everybody in the family wants it. I've always hated computers but now I use it whenever I can. Writing during war is not like writing during peace, though for me it's always been a biological necessity, a way of easing the pain of living.

Today Primakov, the Russian foreign minister, is in Belgrade. I dare not hope. The café in my neighborhood isn't called New York anymore but Baghdad Café.

**The allies reject Milosevic's offer to pull back from Kosovo if NATO agrees to stop air strikes.**

### 31 March

Is it possible that we are all going to be sacrificed for somebody's lack of political judgement, or worse, madness? The conflict is escalating; atrocities are mounting daily. Women from feminist groups and NGOs are rescuing Albanian women and their families from Pristina in flames and terror, risking their lives, as usual...

### 1 April

We spent last night in a shelter, three grown-ups, five children, and two dogs. Actually, it's a private house with a good cellar next to the underground station where I spent the first night of bombing. According to CNN, downtown Belgrade was supposed to be bombed but it wasn't, so once again we wait. Three American soldiers were captured by the Yugoslav army. It was on CNN. This is a dirty, dirty war—frightened people in basements, bruised soldiers on television, Albanian refugees crying on camera, saying things people should never have to say, especially on TV. Human dignity is at stake here for all of us.

My friend, a half-Albanian, half-Serbian Yugoslav, phoned from New York. I am living on European time here, she says. I wish I were there with you, I tell her. We are living on American time, awake at night and dozing during the day. You could say we were living in both time zones at once.

One thing I've noticed: every evening at dusk my hands start to tremble uncontrollably. It goes on for a few hours. I heard that some other women have the same symptoms. It's fear of air raids after dark. The men behave differently. They shout and argue about life and death. We're more afraid of their deaths than our own. Only at certain moments, when I'm struck by images of violence against my children, I feel faint with fear. I think I would prefer suicide.

My parents, alone in their flat, can hardly hear the siren. They watch state TV and they phone me every now and then saying, "Don't worry, it will be OK." And I feel better. Just like when I was a child, my father's voice makes me feel secure. But I don't give that kind of security to my children. It's my deliberate choice not to; the world is *not* a safe place.

I heard that the French, German, American cultural centers in the middle of Belgrade have been completely destroyed by a mob of vandals. I've got no wish to go and examine the ruins, which, like a public corpse, we are invited to witness as a warning.

Some Yugoslav pilots were honored on television by our president; now we see in the paper on the obituary page that they are dead.

## 2 April

Today is Catholic Good Friday and people are getting mystical because of the bombs. They see portents everywhere, in the pattern of days, in the clouds that prevent air strikes, as if they were celestial signs of destiny. Another blow to the common sense of ordinary people.

My friend's son phoned from the battlefield last night. He couldn't say where he was, he just said he was OK but that some of his friends were not. The age limit for volunteers has been raised to seventy-five for men. On CNN, Arkan, the indicted war criminal, is promising lawful and merciful treatment of the three American soldiers. I watch the sea of refugees being marshaled by both sides on the borders with Yugoslavia, Macedonia and Albania. It reminds me of 1995, when Serbs from Krajina poured into Serbia for days with no real idea of what was happening to them.

**NATO targets its bombing campaign on Belgrade.**

## 3 April

It is morning, a beautiful sunny morning, and I am crying. Last night the center of Belgrade was bombed with appalling precision; sure, they hit military targets, but only twenty meters from one of the biggest maternity hospitals in the Balkans, the one where I was born and where I had my baby. The Ministry of the Interior was destroyed; some of my friends remember being interrogated there. I am pleased by NATO's accuracy. But I feel at the mercy of those young pilots, responsible for hitting military targets without harming a single newborn baby.

I heard from a friend who lives in a small village on the Danube near Belgrade that the peasants there are looking for a missing American pilot. They have organized themselves into a guerrilla group like the partisans sixty years ago. My friend said they are probably doing the same thing in villages all over Yugoslavia. "What would you do to the pilot if you found him?" I asked them at home. Nothing, of course, they all said. Some would give him food and preach about the situation in Serbia—mostly the grown-ups; while the children would feed him and hide him in a cellar.

On the BBC, CNN, Sky News, commentators are already talking about the war as a chess game. What a virtual, playful, cruel war. Personally, my war is made up of terrible pictures in my imagination, of my loved ones being killed, tortured, raped. These are the images that haunt me when the siren goes off, this is what is turning my hair white. The first time I got gray hair was ten years ago when a drunken customs officer harassed us at the Slovenian border because we were Serbs. I knew then it was only the beginning. I feel solidarity with anybody who has ever lived through a war—we receive e-mails from such people all over the world.

I am supposed to go to Budapest with my daughter to settle some business matters and to work as if there weren't a war. I keep thinking that perhaps we shouldn't come back until the bombing stops. I don't know how to pack our suitcases—for two days or two years. I wonder if the roads will be safe and who will I be able to turn to when we get there. In '92, when I was a refugee in Vienna, I was overwhelmed with problems, frozen bank accounts, an almost impossible visa regime, and not even the meanest jobs available. It was more than I could bear. I ran back home. I couldn't stand that kind of exile anymore. It's too degrading for my daughter. I prefer hunger and danger which, at least, keeps you vital.

## 4 April

Again a night in the shelter. Two more bridges have been hit and the railway line to Montenegro has been destroyed by SFOR [NATO-led Stabilization Force] troops in Bosnia. The wire is finally visible around our cage. We're bad, wild Serbs from the fourteenth century, disguised in jeans, speaking English, but still aliens... This NATO viewpoint is completely in line with the local nationalists, who said that when the maternity hospital shook from nearby bombing, the babies didn't even cry because they were Serb babies. Well, I cried like a baby yesterday when I heard thousands of people on the Square of the Republic singing "Tamo daleko" ("There, far away is Serbia...") during the daily concert. It's a beautiful old song which Serbian soldiers sang in the First World War on their way to Thessalonika. Only a few came back, and my grandfather was one of them. He used to sing it to me when I was a child, and I always sang it when people abroad asked me for a Serbian song. It always makes people cry. But I couldn't sing yesterday—it's not my song anymore, it's not my Serbia. I am in exile in my own country.

I am supposed to get forty liters of petrol per month, but I have nowhere to go, so maybe I will exchange it for forty liters of wine and forty packs of cigarettes, which are impossible to buy. Maybe this is the route to my Serbia now.

My parents are only fifteen minutes away by foot, but since the war started I haven't managed to see them. Their street seems distant and dangerous. Is this how we are going to live now, divided into separate districts like countries? I watched an officer at the NATO press conference looking at the map of Belgrade and pointing where they are going to strike. He said, "Belgrade is a lovely city. I used to go there often."

## 5 April

In the pharmacy the shelves were more full than ever, except for aspirin or tranquilizers—which is what everybody's been asking for. People are buying sweets like mad—for emotional distress, lack of love.

## 6 April

Today is the anniversary of the Nazi bombing of Belgrade in 1941, but the major damage to the city was done at the end of the war by Allied bombing, and I know everybody will use the parallel to make themselves feel better or worse. This morning I was sitting on the terrace , the sun bathing me with great love. I was dreaming of the sea, and the sky was clear as it was last night when we waited for air raids. The planes came, but they didn't bomb Belgrade. I feel more guilty than ever this morning. People from all over the world ask me, "Do you realize how terrible it is in Kosovo?" I do, I really do, and I feel guilty that we feel sorry for ourselves without living through the horror they do. But our war, whether for the past ten or fifty years, has always been lived in invisible horror. We have a long way to go to be free.

## 7 April

Running to the shelter with food, running out of the shelter to buy food. Phoning friends and relatives, exchanging fears: what, where, when was hit? Who will be next? Never a why. I don't watch the news anymore. I hate all sides equally. Yugoslavia is crumbling, what a pity for all those bridges. Bridges have such nice connotations—

people building them, crossing them. What a pity for all those wasted innocent lives. Is this our future, running in and out of a shelter like a rat? The schools are closed, the children wear the serious eyes of adults. In and out of the shelters. Is this our future?

## 8 April

Last night we sat on the terrace making bets. After a few big explosions, I went deaf in my right ear. A government administration building was hit in downtown Belgrade, only half a mile away. Nobody really knows why that building and not the general headquarters, as was expected. Nobody tells us anything. Was it a civil or military target? Anyway, good, we're done with that. We've been waiting for it for days. We started laughing with relief when we heard there was no "collateral damage," as NATO calls the dead, by the "criminal aggressors," as TV Serbia calls NATO. My father phoned. His voice was trembling, he heard nothing, he saw nothing, he is already deaf and too old to move, but he kept asking: "What can we do now? Nothing, can we? I thought it was the pans falling in the kitchen but then it was bombs. What can we do now?"

Last night the daily concert moved to the bridge over the Sava that joins new and old Belgrade. Our families are split between the two sides but we don't dare cross over to visit in case the bridges are destroyed while we're away.

I watched a BBC military commentator talking about Serbs as horrible people who cared about nothing but their own lives. I hate this kind of ethnic generalization. I never felt there was something like a "British people," even though I spent twelve years in an English-speaking boarding school. But after his remark, I did. I wonder what British people would be like in these conditions?

My old friend Mica, the gypsy woman from the basement, has been rather stable since the bombings started. Her only distress seems to come from the fact that we can't buy cigarettes anymore. She asks me for one every time I pass. She speaks calmly, no more foul language. The difference between us, a white girl and a gypsy girl, is marginal now. We both live in basements with too many emotions, too few cigarettes, and too much beer.

**9 April**
I remember, shortly before the war, today was considered a good date to conceive if you wanted a child to be born on the first day of January, 2000. I remember how silly and ridiculous this seemed; I also remember how suggestive it was. Now the day has arrived and nobody here has any such plans. With all the talk about ground troops entering Yugoslavia, women are hoping they are not pregnant, or wondering what to do with their children if they have to take up arms. Already two of my girlfriends,

pacifists, feminists, said that if it comes to an all-out ground war, they will take up guns instead of staying at home and waiting to be killed, raped, or sent into exile.

Military logic is entering our everyday language. We talk about adapting to war conditions. I thought of starting a school for the children who are suddenly on the loose, without their usual studying routine. Most of us don't go into hiding anymore, don't think of leaving the country. We are just here—who cares for how long?—we are held hostages by our lives. We have no decent way out.

## 10 April

The hairdresser next door is working his usual hours despite the alarm that went off in broad daylight. The pilots were probably frustrated last night, unable to drop their bombs because of the weather. The NATO briefing will be tense, no doubt, but we had a peaceful night: no boom-booms, only local aircraft which at least have a more humane sound, like planes used to have.

Tomorrow is Orthodox Easter. My daughter painted eggs—not that we're religious, but she said she was bored and I thought, better let her do something constructive rather than sulk alone in her room waiting for the sirens to go off. She is a child of the war now. She said yesterday, "I have a feeling I'm going to be killed when I'm sixteen, so what's the point of going to school anymore?"

I froze and said, "You'll go to school anyway."

## 11 April

Last night at midnight Belgrade was in the streets, the sirens were going, but still people crowded into churches for the Easter service. I looked at them: the old, simple and ragged people, the young and middle-aged and better off, and then the minority who are true believers. They all wore the same tragic expression, like a crowd scene from La Scala. At the same time, the rock concert was raging on the Sava bridge, packed with patriots who believe fervently in their own power rather than God's. I don't fit on either side. I don't believe in God but I don't believe in myself, not with the world the way it is.

I don't want my children to take any risks when the sirens go off, so I went to the video club and took out some films for us. One was a Mickey Rourke film—my favorite actor until eighteen days ago—but he seemed so foolish. I thought, he knows nothing about me anymore. So Mickey Rourke and I had to split after all these years.

I went to bed early and slept like a log. The fridge makes a terrible row, worse than air raids, so I decided to switch it off and clean it today, even though my granny used to say it was bad luck to work on Easter Day.

When I was five my grandmother took me to church on Easter, secretly, so that my communist parents wouldn't know. I remember my excitement upon entering the biggest building I had ever been in, full of strange smells and glimmering candles. After that first moment of joy, I was overcome by a feeling which comes over me to this day when entering a church: the feeling of power-lessness, of the invisibility of my little person. I started crying like crazy, saying to my granny, "I will be burned, I will be punished..." So she had to take me out, much distressed by her failed mission. I remember she bought me an ice cream and a toy dog, and we never spoke about Easter or church again. It was years before I went into another church, and the feeling was pretty the same, but my mystical crisis was over—not resolved, but ended—and by that time my granny was no longer around to comfort me or try to explain.

## 12 April

I couldn't get to sleep last night so finally I took a tran-quilizer—there, I've started too. All these weeks I've put off using drugs to stay sane, but I realize that it's impos-sible to stay sane in Belgrade without them. I understand those who leave. I could have been one of them, but I don't want to leave my city, my friends, my language. Friends from all over the world offer me flats, money, help, but the only thing I need from them is to try to stop our war.

Yesterday, Slavko Curuvija, a newspaper editor, was shot in front of his house in the center of Belgrade in the middle of the day. Who's going to be next?

The kids go to discotheques and hold parties during the day. They say it may be their last bit of fun.

More factories were destroyed last night, more fuel dumps, in Pancevo and Novi Sad, two towns which for the past few years have been full of Serbian refugees from Croatia and Bosnia. I have friends in both. One of them e-mailed me: "Yes we will go on with work for our international summer schools, they are more important than ever. But at the moment we have dead people here, though we in the peace movement are still all alive." He's a better person than I am. I don't want to fake normal life.

Last night the old man next door was taken to hospital during the air raids. He was tied to a chair and carried out of his flat. "Good night," he said politely. I guess it was some kind of nervous breakdown. Alone all these weeks, he couldn't take it anymore. He'll be better off in a crowded hospital.

**NATO planes hit a civilian passenger
train near Leskovac, south of Belgrade.
Ten people are killed.**

## 13 April

The old man next door died. "Good night ladies, good night my sweet ladies..." Today a woman who sustained facial injuries when NATO bombed a train was asked on TV: "What do you think of this NATO aggression?"

She said, "I was just going to visit my relatives for Easter."

I saw doctors and family members on buses leaving Belgrade for the place where the train was hit on a bridge. Nobody was crying or showing emotion. I caught sight of my own reflection in a window. I have changed, too. I don't cry anymore. I sleep during the raids. I work during the day. I laugh. When you get used to war, you forget to ask how and why.

**An Albanian refugee convoy on a road outside Prizren in southern Kosovo is hit by NATO planes. At least seventy-two people are killed.**

### 15 April

In the middle of the night, the windows started to rattle like in a horror movie and the sky was lit up by fire. My daughter woke up screaming and clung to me. She is bigger than I am now, but suddenly she seemed like a little baby. I was so exhausted I could hardly open my eyes. She was afraid but she didn't want to go down to the shelter. She asked, "What's happening, what's all the noise...?"

"It's our anti-aircraft, darling, don't be afraid," I said. It was the first time since the war started that I made a distinction between "our" weapons and "their" weapons.

But it was only to calm her, not because I believe in the distinction.

Yesterday, more than a thousand people attended the funeral of Slavko Curuvija, the newspaper editor who was found with three bullets in the back of his head, the mark of a contract killing. The more I hear, the less I am convinced there is any story to it at all, other than that he was a brave, intelligent, powerful, good-looking man. I guess that was enough.

Horrible, horrible pictures of refugees in a convoy in Kosovo hit by NATO bombs. Horrible NATO definition of "collateral damage to the targeted military convoy." I saw some soldiers here in Belgrade. They were young, very worried, awkwardly carrying their big guns. I can imagine them in a convoy during the night in the woods in Kosovo. Any of these city boys could be my son.

## 16 April

Last night our household exploded in panic. The noises and lights of the Yugoslav anti-aircraft covered the sky over Belgrade while literally three hundred NATO planes flew over the city. The children started screaming, out of terror and joy, as if they were at the circus. I rushed them down to our local shelter, gulping down some wine to stop my hands and knees from trembling, and then after half an hour we went back home, where the children say they feel best. We slept like logs.

People have no money to buy anything, and those who have some are keeping it for the future. The shops are full and the prices are going down, especially for clothes. Yesterday, we went shopping. We called it the Last Shopping.

We heard on the radio that children no longer have to pass a state exam to get into high school. They're overjoyed—no exams, no school, nothing. They say, "Don't you see now, going to school was useless? The things that matter are power and money." They don't associate knowledge with power and money, not after this war.

People from abroad ask me how Serbian people are taking the deaths of the bombed refugees. What a question. The same as all other civilian deaths, of which there have been too many already in this "humanitarian bombing." It never occurred to me to think of dead civilians as Albanians or Serbs. But obviously people from NATO countries feel differently. I suppose they paid for the bombs with their taxes, so maybe they're allowed to choose their victims. Let's hope that "humanitarian" bombs really bring us peace, and not just the peace of death.

## 17 April

An American journalist on TV quoted an Australian aid worker in Kosovo saying, "Thanks NATO for bombing us, for destroying our blankets and medicines." To which a NATO officer at the press conference replied: "Sorry but our maps are old." A peasant woman who sells home-made cheese at the market said to me: "They're bombing the hell out of us, everything is destroyed. Can't some-body tell them that it's been two years now since the army moved out of our village?" I guess it's the old maps again.

Last night Belgrade was spared from bombs because of the terrible weather. It's raining, the wind is pounding the windows, the panes are rattling, and bits of masonry are falling off the facades of old buildings. I hear more and more stories about people staying in bed watching cartoons on TV. I, on the other hand, am very active, too active, the flip side of depression. I rush about like a robot, anxious that my chores, even the petty ones, are done.


**Thousands of Kosovar Albanians
attempt to cross the borders with
Albania and Macedonia.**


### 18 April

It is Sunday, but who cares? We have been living the same day ever since the war started. In Belgrade there are efforts at normality—the traditional marathon was held in heavy rain; there was a big wedding on TV—but personally, I'm done with anything that resembles human life. I'd rather be a cockroach at this point, much safer.

Last night three factories in Pancevo were hit again, including the chemical factory, where there was an acid leak. Some people are being evacuated. We in Belgrade had a good wind; we were lucky once more. In Batajnica, near the airport, a three-year-old girl was killed by falling glass after an explosion. Her father said she'd been difficult in the night. First she wanted to go to the bathroom, then she didn't, then she did. And then he let her go in and she never came out.

## 19 April

Last night my friends were very pessimistic about the future. They are all educated people, members of the opposition but with more or less strong patriotic feelings who have been impoverished by the last ten years of economic upheaval. They don't want to go into exile. There is an increasingly strong feeling here among ordinary people that nobody really wants us anywhere, not even here. Writers and commentators from all over the world now refer to the Serbs as being accomplices in the atrocities, and they mean all Serbs. I won't name names, but some were people I admired, even friends. I forgive them, but I don't read them. Just as with our local nationalistic writers some years ago; for me, they don't exist.

**Yugoslavia closes its border with Albania, and tens of thousands of refugees are turned back into southern Kosovo.**

## 20 April

Oh, and about the atrocities, about the Albanian refugees? Please, all of you reading this, understand that I accept as much blame as you want me to. I know what is going on, even if I have no more proof than what some people say, just as I am telling you all these things about my life, expecting you to believe me. Which cross should I bear—NATO bombs or Serbian killings? Between compulsive patriotism and compulsive guilt, I guess there is no way out.

## 21 April

Yesterday, the Patriarch of the Russian Orthodox church paid an official visit to Belgrade. We were asked to walk in the streets without party slogans or even flags, each carrying a candle. I decided not to go. Last night, the building which formerly housed the Central Committee of the Communist Party in Novi Beograd was hit.

## 22 April

I drink wine every night in order to get to sleep. I even give it to the children so they can sleep through the explosions.

Last night the president's residence was hit and destroyed: no comment. The government channel shows pictures of the destroyed villa in silence.

## 23 April

I guess you all know, the TV building was hit last night. My windows were blown open by the blast. We live quite near to it, my parents just behind it, and a close friend is in the building next door. We are all OK, but the TV workers sacrificed their lives.

My father said the impact wasn't so bad, the worst part was seeing the decapitated bodies being taken from the building. Some of the foreign journalists who arrived yesterday are afraid for their lives. Today, Serbian TV is broadcasting again, even better than yesterday.

## 24 April

Since the NATO celebration in Washington is dazzling all the TV channels, we expected the bridges in Belgrade to be hit, finished off in one big operation to celebrate the new NATO accord. I watched the military waltzes, the flags, the uniforms, the audience, the speeches—it was as surreal as our lives here. In the end, Belgrade wasn't hit. The siren went off anyway, but I had a good sleep. My friend from Rakovica, a badly damaged part of Belgrade, is afraid of radioactivity. She wants to leave, but all she can do is watch videos while bombs fall around her.

I just heard that the people in the TV building were warned by NATO about the air strikes but apparently decided to follow orders and stay. My guess is not all of them had a free choice.

## 25 April

Last night I watched a film with Jeff Bridges about recovery from posttraumatic shock after a plane crash. I had phobias about dying in a plane crash after surviving an emergency landing of a Swissair flight in 1997 — the same flight crashed a year later in the same place. I developed phobias when NATO threatened to bomb Belgrade in 1992, 1995, and 1998. But I'm not afraid of death anymore. Now, planes bomb us almost every night and my only wish is to die together with those I love.

Politicians here are speaking of all-out war, of Serbian blood being spilled. People are talking about life without water and electricity. Our Bosnian friends are sending us instructions on how to survive. We play with the children all day long to keep them busy and to forget our worries...

Today, after many days, I went out into the streets of Belgrade. I ventured out to take a close look at the bombed building in the city center and at the faces of the passers-by. I was not as impressed as I thought I would be. We sat in a café in front of a destroyed building. It didn't feel particularly strange. But the faces of the people are definitely different, long and worried. I am glad people are finally thinking enough to be worried.

No more state TV. My friend who looks after her very old father said, "Oh my God, what will I do now? Without TV, he cries and refuses to use the toilet."

**26 April**

Today is the anniversary of Chernobyl. I remember how hysterical I was about that disaster. I remember how the government TV broadcasts withheld the truth about the level of radiation in order to "not create panic." I remember walking with my daughter in the rain, which I later learned was extremely radioactive.

The shops are still full but people are talking about radioactive vegetables. They are also predicting a future without bread, water, or electricity. No visible signs of that yet, only fear. We still have shortages of cigarettes and petrol—and, of course, peace.

Today the famous NATO star Jamie Shea announced that we Serbian citizens feel safe with NATO bombs—we don't stop working when we hear the sirens. Well, maybe not, but that's because the work has to be done, not because we feel safe. I don't feel safe with NATO or any other bombs. I don't feel safe without bridges. I don't feel safe in a boat, on a horse, or on a bicycle against a NATO bomber. I don't feel safe without schools, universities, or libraries against highly technological NATO countries.

## 27 April

Last night we got the same program on ten channels; the same news the whole day. Then, on the BBC, I saw my friend Vjosa, an Albanian from Kosovo, a human rights activist and a doctor, describing the horrors she suffered running for her life from Pristina. It made me cry, not so much because of her story, which I already knew, but for her. She has changed so much. Her face had in it something of a person who would never laugh again.

Last night, an enormous blast, as if around the corner. Again, it was the former central committee building across the river. I don't even know what's inside it now, but for some reason when it gets hit you can hear it more than much closer targets. We called our friends and relatives, checked we were alive, and went to bed.

## 28 April

Last night my friend and I were sitting planning the future of our feminist publishing house, 94. The last book we published, *The Origins of Totalitarianism* by Hannah Arendt, appeared two days before the bombing. I wonder what Hannah Arendt would say about being published by feminists in the middle of another European war. We were nervous because it was 1:00 A.M., and there were no sirens. Like many people in Belgrade, we have developed what is called "siren neurosis"—we are always waiting for them to go off. But the explosions started soon enough—

and big ones: windows were blown open, the building shook, fireworks lit up in the sky. First Yugoslav anti-aircraft responded, then the clouds broke open with thunder, lightning, and heavy rain. We all went to sleep together in one big bed with the children's toys and lots of cushions.

The cleaning lady came late this morning. There were no buses, no petrol. She said she spent all night in the shelter; she didn't believe we would win the war anyway. One of my children's friends said to me, "Hurrah! No more music classes, our teacher has become a sniper!" I remember him, a particularly talented student from the Academy. My friend's son who is serving in the regular army phones often. He is afraid and cold, but alive. My friend has stopped eating and laughs all the time.

Then, this morning, we heard that NATO has made another mistake. They have hit a village in southern Serbia, more "collateral damage," this time to children in a "safe" shelter. I wonder how many people in Belgrade go to the shelters anymore? I still see them in front of the entrance every night, smoking and drinking, but I don't know whether they go there to socialize or to find safety.

Petrol has been rationed to twenty liters a month. Petrol prices on the black market have doubled. One bit of good news: on the BBC, I see that the Hungarians might be putting up a refugee camp near Budapest, this time for Serbs, though they will be treated officially as tourists. I feel a bit safer. If we have to leave, we'll be in a camp with people like ourselves, where we can share our fears and where our children can play together.

A friend calls to tell me an ecological catastrophe is on the way. No more vegetables and fruit, only tinned food and bottled water. Reports have been circulating on the internet, documenting the poisoning of air and water. A young friend of mine decided to have an abortion because she believed what they were saying. She's been crying for days.

The alarm again. It's daytime. My daughter phones to say she is coming home. That's our deal, until the war is over we will stay together most of the time.

## 29 April

The washing machine broke down. I wept as if somebody had died. I imagine myself doing all the laundry by hand as well as all the extra housework I've had to do since the war started. Then I remembered hearing how, in NATO Phase Three, we will have no water, no electricity, and no phone lines. I imagine myself with many other women, washing the laundry in the Danube as they did in ancient Greece, singing, gossiping, and laughing, with kids running all around us. That will be my summer holiday.

A friend of mine couldn't meet me because his father had a heart attack from the bombing. I seem to remember, before the first air raids began, the old man saying, "Let them attack us, we will fight back." He scorned his son who didn't want to fight. Now that his son is risking his life to take care of him, I wonder whether the old man's changed his mind.

**30 April**
My friend's son, the soldier, sent a message from somewhere in Kosovo. He wants to marry his girlfriend so she can have his flat legally if he is killed.

Step by step, down, down, every day crossing a new border of horror, yesterday's fear, today's habit. Last night a bomb landed only a hundred meters from us. The blast was so strong, the building shook for minutes and we hung on to each other laughing with nerves. "They'll kill us eventually," somebody said, "either psychologically or physically." Then we all went to bed together. After a few hours there were no more explosions but the shaking went on and on. We hung on to each other half asleep, in silence.

No news on TV. We are still shaking and feeling sick.

Belgrade was never hit so hard before. Dead bodies are lying around the ruined buildings, car alarms from wrecked cars are wailing, and rescue vans are circling with their headlights on. And life goes on—today with no buses or trams, and lettuce, fruit, and vegetables from the market forbidden because the earth has been poisoned with uranium. No information, because it doesn't help anyway.

After thirty-seven days of air strikes, I finally gave in and let my daughter go out during the alarm for only half an hour, but I know now there is no way back. We are determined to enjoy life in any way we can. I'm aware of a strange new sensation creeping up my spine. It's the thrill of risk, of death. Fear of death is not the same as fear of dying: the first is thrilling, the second depressing.

## 1 May

Very soon I won't be able to think about leaving. The last bridges are waiting to fall, and then there'll be no choice.

All of us are living from day to day. When I walk down the street in this beautiful weather and this beautiful city—even in ruins—I watch how people move, I notice the places they choose to rest. Everybody thinks their place is the safest in the world, whether out of superstition or some rationale.

## 2 May

Yesterday, one of the TV stations broadcast a long, untranslated conversation between two Chinese people. I went to the video shop, where a group of people were discussing one of the leaflets which had been dropped all over the city. As far as I could understand, it was a NATO leaflet, in bad Serbian, saying that the war will be over in forty-eight hours when the last bridge over the Danube is hit. We will be an island.

## 3 May

Finally it happened, a blackout, in a city of two and a half million people. It's already lasted sixteen hours, but I think it will last for good. We gathered on the terrace with everything we had gathered for survival without electricity and water. Until the beginning of the war we hardly knew our neighbors, but now we're all in the same boat. We collected water in tubs and bottles, offered books for the fire, and pooled grain and potatoes. We decided to go to bed with the sun at eight in the evening and hold survival meetings every morning. When will this end? For most people bets are off, the war should have ended already. I guessed June 2. Everybody felt relieved.

This morning, some areas have got their light and water back, but not ours. I am here at my friend's table with my portable computer. The children are baking bread. Tomorrow we've been told the phone lines and the last bridges will be destroyed. I want to say goodbye to so many people and in the end I say goodbye to no one.

We've been buying church candles because they last longer and are cheaper; we buy batteries for radios, simple food and plain water. No cigarettes, no alcohol. We've fished out old clothes and rearranged the furniture to suit life in the dark—so we don't trip over it. All of Belgrade is doing the same thing.

**4 May**

Yesterday was a beautiful day, with no electricity, no water. People had despair in their eyes, as if they had no idea what to do with themselves. It's not just the bombs, it's this pointless passing of time which destroys us. There are problems with the children, the small ones cry all the time, the big ones are angrier and more spoiled than ever. They can't—don't want to—understand the war. This lack of a bridge between generations is our fault. We didn't want to poison them with stories of the old wars, and now they are living a new one without any idea of what it means.

The man who came to help me move the furniture asked for a glass of water. I said, of course. After drinking it he said, "Please, be so kind and give me another one." It was only then I realized that he must have come from an area of the city that has no water.

"Please, take a bath, whatever, we have water. This is a criminal war," I said.

He looked at me and said, "But we will win."

I didn't realize that there are still people who still think of this existence as a victory.

**5 May**

Last night I went to bed early and lay awake in the dark alone. I realized I hadn't had a chance to be alone since the bombing began. It's raining, we have no electricity, but no bombs either. It's no use writing because of the blackouts. I heard on the BBC that we were without light for only six or seven hours, but that's not true. I don't know whose propaganda it is, local or foreign, but it doesn't help us believe news about the Albanians, from either side, when we hear that we have electricity and water because it suits somebody's purpose to say so. All the news suits somebody.

I'm constantly running from one flat to another with my computer, my meatballs, and the laundry, running after electricity. But I feel as if I'm bringing bad luck. As soon as I arrive the lights go out; the moment I leave to go to another flat that has electricity, the lights come back on. It's like when you queue in one line and the other moves faster. You can't win. I'm running like the Masai—I heard they never walk, or stop, except to sleep or die.

### 6 May
Everybody I talk to has left, is leaving, or has a safe place to go. I don't. I desperately belong to this falling city. We change flats for the night, fantasizing which will be safer, what will be hit, as I am sure everybody does. It is a game we play, a game for rats.

### 7 May
Today is my parents' fiftieth wedding anniversary. We had planned a surprise party, but yesterday they said they

were sick and couldn't have any guests. Who knows what it is like to measure out your marriage with bombs at either end? The second and third largest cities in Yugoslavia have been hit hard. In Nis, where some of my relatives live, the central market has been destroyed. Many civilians are dead. A Sky News journalist reports the deaths. NATO knows nothing about it. Of course, it's true. It reminds me of when the people queuing for bread were killed in the marketplace in Sarajevo. Was it Serbs or was it Muslims who fired the shell? The debate went on for years.

## 8 May

A friend in the computer business who lives next to the Chinese Embassy had her windows blown out, and shrapnel flew into her room. I phoned her as soon as I heard what the target was.

"Do you know what we call windows in Belgrade?" she asked. All our windows are broken and crisscrossed with scotch tape. "WINDOWS 99."

## 9 May

I slept for thirteen hours because there were no bombs; tonight I am sure there'll be many. I feel like a battered woman who expects violence and then feels loved if the punch misses her.

Last night, once again, we sat on the terrace, drank wine, smoked nasty, expensive cigarettes, and fantasized about the future. Since we have none, we're free to dream up anything. I've never had such wild ambitions as these nights on the terrace. I even offered to lead the country out of war, if my refugee friend from Krajina agrees to be the Minister of Finance and my best friend from the women's center the Minister of Police.

I'd like to say something about the bombing of the Chinese Embassy. Of course it was a mistake, a grossly incompetent mistake. But a mistake nonetheless, which happens in all wars. But what a lot of noise about it. What about all the others killed while sleeping in their beds, buying food at the market, or drinking wine on the terrace, looking at the starry sky above? They are also people who died for no reason.

## 10 May

I thought I should have some kind of escape plan in case I go crazy and start doing strange things, so I'm trying to get an Italian visa. After days of long and complicated negotiations, with generous help from my Italian friend, the visa department in the Italian Embassy was hit. My papers are lost, along with my shattered hopes. Always too late, my usual script.

I went out to my car, which I haven't done for over a month now, and I turned on the radio. They were playing old songs, "April in Belgrade," "Green, Green Eyes of Yours," and suddenly I burst into tears. I had to pull over because my sight was blurred. I was sobbing out loud. Calm down, I told myself, you're a reasonable person, control yourself. You never even liked that music; you never even liked to drive a car. Yes, came back the thought, but what I loved was the life I lost, and part of that was the luxury of despising sentimental music and big cars. I was overcome by a terrible sense of loss, as if I'd been killed by accident and somebody else had stepped into my skin and taken over my life.

Yesterday, I heard one of the worst stories I've heard since the beginning of the war. A young man, dealing in gold—but not a criminal—came across a dead person's teeth filled with gold. In order to get the gold, he had to crush the teeth. He did it and then threw up. He didn't want think about the fate of the person whose teeth were in his hands. He said, "Lately the price of gold has gone down a lot in Belgrade because there are so many Albanian jewels around." I felt a terrible toothache at that moment. Hardly anyone has gold teeth anymore, but I do, from a visit to an Italian dentist when I was sixteen.

## 11 May

I passed a thin, young girl of about fifteen on the street. She seemed very self-conscious and shy—the tortures of adolescence. I looked at her longer than I should have because I was thinking about my own daughter and myself at that age. Then suddenly a blast shook the ground. In a second she changed from a beautiful girl into a frightened animal. She put her hands to her throat as if somebody was choking her, then to her heart, and then she fainted. I ran up. I had an urge to kiss her as I often do to my daughter to wake her up, but people gathered round and carried her to a restaurant where she could lie down and take some water.

Our children got their grades today, officially no more school. One of my daughter's best friends went to Australia with her parents some years ago when the situation here began to get worse. Now they have a house on the sea and she has become a model, while my daughter is here, burdened with our history and fighting for her life. She has grown old very quickly, though part of her is still a child, like the girl on the street. She and her friend in Australia stopped writing to each other because they no longer had anything in common.

## 12 May

I'm running through the city like crazy, collecting documents to prove I am myself. I'm also doing this for members of my family so we can get visas. In the meantime, I hear that a bridge on the border with Hungary was hit last night, and that Hungarian customs officers are armed, searching people, and demanding bribes as the mood strikes them. Of course, if you are a man, you need a special permit to leave the country. The siren goes on night and day.

## 13 May

Besides a lack of cigarettes, which has produced interminable queues curling like snakes around the buildings, street corners, parks, wherever they sell them, we now lack laundry detergent. Actually, you can find it on the black market, like cigarettes, doubled in price.

I just heard on Sky News how Serb men fight differently from British and other soldiers. How stupid that is, racism, militarism, and sexism all rolled into one. Serb soldiers are just as good or bad as any others. They watch the same Bruce Willis films, drive the same cars, dream of Pamela Anderson.

# PART THREE

*Political Idiots*

1999

Every evening we go to the shelter in my local underground station. I know people there. We try to make plans and watch the news, none of it good, none of it reliable. The gypsies and the adolescents are the most frightened. The gypsies have been persecuted for centuries; the adolescents want their lives back.

## 14 May

In order to get a visa for Italy, you must have a new passport, and you can't get a passport because the computer system is down in the police station. Even if you had a passport, you couldn't get a visa because the system is down at the Italian Embassy. But if you cross the border and go to Budapest, and you have a lot of money for bribes, hotels, food, and can afford days and days of waiting, you might get a visa and a new passport.

Nearly impossible to find an empty cab, or one whose passengers are willing to share it with you. On the cab radio, I heard that refugees had been hit again and that the military barracks where sons of my friends are stationed had also been bombed. I just couldn't listen to the news anymore. I said, "Stop the car." I don't know why. The cab driver stopped, and the man next to him screamed, "You can't do this to me! I'm in a hurry!" I grabbed the handle to open the door, and the driver shouted, "Not that way…" I opened the door, and a big red car nearly killed me. The driver of the car blew his horn, but I didn't see him until he was nearly on top of me. Nobody slows down these days.

## 15 May

I watched a program on TV about a woman who works as a registrar for marriages in central Belgrade. There are many more marriages in war than in peace — soldiers off to the front; young people, deeply in love, going straight from the shelters to get married; pregnant women, sometimes with nothing but a piece of paper from their husband-to-be.

Alarms all night, but no bombs. In the city at night, it's completely dark. You step into puddles, dog shit, vomit, and gobs of spit (my pet obsession). But otherwise people play their loud music, dance before the windows in candlelight, and sit out on their doorsteps close to the cellar, watching the low-flying planes. Exactly six hundred seventy-five last night.

I've noticed a new common phenomenon here, sleepwalkers. We meet people, even in this building, talking to themselves, and then in the morning, they can't remember what happened and where they went.

## 16 May

Last night the planes nearly flew right in through the windows, followed by the local anti-aircraft defense guns. We have this beautiful, typical old-fashioned Belgrade window, overlooking a courtyard. These courtyards are like small alternative communities sheltered by high walls. They're mostly populated by gypsies or people who live as if they were still in the country. They have vegetable patches and outdoor toilets. Those of us who have flats overlooking the courtyards see and hear them, but the people below don't see or hear us. I was born in such a flat, in downtown Belgrade. Years later, when I saw my present flat, I fell in love with it because it reminded me of my childhood. From the courtyards, we have a clear view of the sky and the low-flying planes that seem like birds who might swoop into our rooms.

My daughter says, "This war will never end. I can't sleep in my room because of the planes."

"Of course it will end; all wars end," I tell her. But what comes after is no better, I think, poverty and isolation.

The Italian Embassy is no longer willing to give us visas. Well, that's my punishment for procrastinating.

**17 May**
A friend's two-year-old daughter runs around the house all day saying "I won't give up Kosovo, I won't give up Kosovo." Her father can't do anything with her, all she wants to do is watch TV.

Everybody is talking about the general mobilization scheduled for 24 May. There is slightly more panic and tension in the air. I wonder what's going on in people's heads; probably the same mess I'm writing about, more or less well articulated. One of my friends said there was an incredible number of decent people in this country but they were incapable of organizing themselves into a party to work together. So we are a country without opposition, a country with no leaders but one, a country of political idiots like me.

## 20 May

We were watching a video interview with our Albanian friend who described her escape from Pristina. She talked about us, too, and how she had received support from her friends in Belgrade rather than from her Serb neighbors. Then missiles started flying above our heads, followed by lots of explosions, but we went on listening to our friend's horrors, living in Blace camp in no-man's-land, along with a hundred thousand other refugees, before she finally crossed the border. It was peculiar. We had made a silent decision to put solidarity with our friends before our own survival, as if that could help in some way. Our children said nervously, "Stop watching that stuff. Turn it off." And in the end, I lost my concentration, there were too many bombs; a hospital was hit, among other buildings, and a chemical factory. Yesterday, a bunch of nationalists attacked the Democratic Party headquarters just around the corner, calling their leader—who is in exile in Montenegro—a traitor. He's a handsome middle-aged man who speaks several languages, with a beautiful wife and two children. Now he's fighting on two fronts, against NATO and in a civil war.

## 21 May

A complete blackout over most of Serbia. I managed to get a new passport for my daughter, and a new identity card, the first in her young life. "Wow," she said, "I'm a big girl now." Someone should pay for her sudden rise to adulthood, but I won't live long enough to see it, I'm sure of that.

Deserters are leaving the battlefield. If I were a mother of a soldier sent against his will to fight by white-haired patriots sitting in Belgrade, I would buy a gun and kill all those responsible, giving my life in exchange for my child's. Watching my Albanian friend's interview, I realized how perverse it was, our crying over her life story, indifferent to planes above our heads. We are just a step behind the Albanians—but if we decided to leave, nobody would take us.

My local market used to be a happy place, full of gypsies, peasants, secondhand stalls, smugglers, with police chasing those of us who were buying illegal stuff (though not too fast because they did the same thing privately), but now it's become really ugly. Just when we intellectuals have stopped talking politics, the people in the market have started. I heard this morning there were more than two sides to the war: NATO, Milosevic, and now Djindjic, the leader of the Democratic Party in exile. So now we have more than two options—at least in the marketplace of ideas. The woman I buy eggs from said: "Yes, we have still everything except happiness." Her son is fighting in Kosovo, and she hadn't heard from him for weeks. She didn't even cry, she just had a hard sadness in her face.

## 23 May

We were shooting a film of my diary in the street, and it seemed everybody wanted to be in it, even the policemen we were hiding the cameras from. Some people are angry with NATO, some with the local leaders, some with the whole world. But they all see the pointless situation they are in, and they just want to survive to tell us about it. We're all the same, we fear isolation more than bombs.

We have been without electricity for more than twenty-four hours now. Some people don't even have water. There is absolutely nothing we can do. I phone my parents. They tell me, don't worry, the Russians will give us electricity. They always manage to placate me with fairy stories, just like when I was a child.

## 24 May

Mostly without electricity and water. Every day, I say I must learn how to bake bread, and then I read and write instead. This morning, the children didn't want to get out of bed because there is nothing to do. I proposed that we repair the electrical wiring during the day, and then NATO will hit it again by night. That's the game. It is not important who wins, the point is to play. And water? Well that's a more serious matter. My friend with the disabled, dying father said she would rather die with him than take care of him without water. My American friend in Hungary saw smugglers with thousands of packs of

Pampers heading towards Serbia. "How can you defeat NATO with Pampers?" she asked me. I said, we'll all need Pampers soon. But at least here in Belgrade we are slowly getting angry with ourselves for being political idiots. My taxi driver, a middle-aged man who was an engineer and lost his job said, "We deserve it."

## 25 May

We were trying to film at the Tito Museum on Tito's official birthday—it used to be called the Holiday of Youth—and I was feeling young and carefree like I used to twenty years ago when I was a filmmaker, when I suddenly realized it was noon, the alarm was on, and I had no idea where my daughter was. My husband was somewhere on the border on his way back from a PEN conference in Slovenia. During the night, central Belgrade had been hit again, only a hundred meters from where we were standing. It was a terrible feeling. I had wanted to make this film with my friends to remember those things we will immediately forget as soon as we get the chance. We are building a memorial to fear with our film.

## 26 May

Today we went to film in a very dangerous zone near a part of Belgrade which is hit on a regular basis. The siren was going and a military car pulled up next to us. Before we could show our permits, they pointed their guns at us.

I thought I would faint. But they were very polite and explained that they were just doing their duty. Finally, they advised us to go away. I thought I must be crazy to do this. Why am I doing it? But, then, how can we stay rational if everybody has gone crazy? The politics of high risk, as my husband puts it, have deteriorated into the politics of absolute risk.

This afternoon we went to a restaurant on a boat on the Danube. It's a beautiful place where we used to spend a fortune for few hours of bliss. The food is still good but no seafood—yes, we've lost the sea. There was hardly anybody there, and the restaurant closed at 7:00 P.M., so there wasn't a chance to regain any sense of being an ordinary person.

Doctors are advising women in the early months of pregnancy to have an abortion. I don't know whether this is medical advice, because of radiation, or political-economic advice. One doctor said it's what she would say to her daughter. I also heard on the BBC that a thousand babies have been born in refugee camps in Macedonia. So life goes on, thank God.

**27 May**
Very heavy raids last night. The phone kept ringing, we were checking whether our family and friends were OK, what targets had been hit. At a certain point, I realized I was sleeping between phone calls without hearing the

bombs. The place where we filmed yesterday was hit by twenty-five missiles only a few hours after we left it.

## 28 May

Again, no electricity, a little bit of water, but good weather, sunny and a full moon. Our president has been indicted for war crimes, but the American officials say they will still negotiate with him.

## 29 May

We filmed a sequence for our movie in the Zoo: jailed, hungry, nervous animals. The animals sense danger before we do, especially the peacocks. The director told us that the night downtown Belgrade was heavily bombed, some mothers ate their young—wolves, tigers, and some of the birds.

My friend says that our film stocks are being destroyed because of the heat and the lack of electricity. And I thought of all our unwritten, unpublished books, and those scattered in our damaged flats and garages all over the city. We are losing our intellectual history in this war, along with everything else.

## 30 May

Another nervous day full of heat and alarms. The official daily *Politika* has named some intellectuals in the opposition as traitors. I hear terrible things about what is going on in Kosovo, both from people going in and those coming out. My feminist friend wants to organize a women's peace demonstration in Belgrade, and I'm supporting her, but I wonder if it will do any good—maybe we shouldn't wonder, just do it as a matter of course. Families I know are talking about leaving again; those who left are coming back, either because they ran out of money or because their visas expired. All I know is I can't stand bombs and winter together; something will have to happen.

## 31 May

In the local market, good-looking women glance furtively over their shoulders as policemen in cars point angry fingers at them. You would think they were prostitutes, but they are cigarette smugglers.

All Belgrade is talking about the NATO flyers announcing the bridge targets. Belgrade is targeted now day and night. It is hard to restrain young people. They despise and disobey us...I am in a panic.

My friend who is looking after her dying father is optimistic. She says he is completely dependent on her. She does all the dirty work, but she feels fine, after all these years she is finally in charge. She has defeated him.

## 2 June

I remember more than a month ago when we were betting on the date of the end of the war, I said 2 June for no particular reason. Today is the day. Last night, after midnight, we got electricity after twenty-four hours in the dark. We were listening eagerly to Radio Free Europe by candlelight. When the power came on, we didn't turn to CNN, because foreign broadcasts don't talk about us anymore, though I had a feeling that maybe this would be the day.

My Italian friend asked, "So you don't have bread, light, water, but you sound in good shape?" I am, I said. I can't remember myself some weeks ago when I was so unhappy. Most people turn their backs on people in trouble, but only some, not all. If this horror is worth anything, it is meeting those few people and seeing what humanity is made of.

We are getting so bored that we can hardly put up with each other any longer. There is nothing to do. Our children are fighting us for not letting them go out during the bombing and for having nothing to do when darkness comes. I say let's talk, we've forgotten how to tell each other stories, to amuse each other as people used to. But for them, sitting in the dark with their parents sounds like utter defeat. So they cry or sulk, depending how old they are.

My father went to the bank to pay his electricity and water bills, which nobody pays anymore. He said, "We must help the state in this catastrophe." The bank teller was furious. She told him: "You foolish old man, keeping me here while the siren is on so you can spend your last penny.

Can't you change, see what your stupid obedience has brought to us all?" My father was deeply offended, as he often is nowadays when people don't pay him the respect he feels he's due as a retired general manager who once had power. But he said to me: "I understand her, even though it is not right. A state is a state—my father served under the Austro-Hungarian empire and he did what he had to do."

**Milosevic accepts NATO terms for peace.**

### 3 June
Was all this really necessary? Today, bedridden, frightened, impoverished, faithless if not dead.

### 5 June
A storm last night instead of bombs, thunder, heavy, oily drops of rain. No euphoria on the streets. People are exhausted, bewildered, disappointed. During the storm, I walked through Belgrade. The windows were lit up and loud music was playing as if the dark times and silence were over. But people are still afraid to voice their opinions. They still talk quietly and only to their closest friends. It's not clear who is the winner, but it's clear that we are the losers. We knew that beforehand, so let's get it over with.

My daughter got top grades at school, even though she's hardly been there. I wonder what her grades would have been if she had. She seems to be about five years older than when the bombing started. She seems older than me and treats me as if she is. I've lost her.

**Serb military leaders refuse to withdraw from Kosovo. NATO continues air strikes against Yugoslavia.**

### 6 June

A lot of tension in the air. You can see it on people's faces, there have been accidents and quarrels. During the bombings, it was the opposite. So now we have to endure a collective nervous breakdown, fits of rage and tears, punishment and self-punishment.

A friend of mine phoned me last night from somewhere in Kosovo. He is a soldier. He knew nothing of the deal in Macedonia, nor did anybody in his regiment. He said to me, we all want NATO to win quickly so we can go back home. But it's all over, I said. He made me repeat myself several times.

We are waiting for news. I wake up very early in the morning to watch the news, as I did when the deal over the Dayton Treaty was being negotiated. There are so many dates, so many treaties; this war has been going on nearly all my adult life, certainly all of my daughter's life. My stepson said it wasn't so bad after all, he just hoped we never went back to what it was like before the bombings. I doubt that will happen, so maybe it's been worthwhile. Young people are stronger and smarter than I am. I would give all the power in the world to anyone who was under thirty and had never ruled before. But I must admit, today I felt life and hope running through my veins. I felt alive and confident, the way you feel at the beginning of a new love affair.

### 7 June

I spent the night listening to the news, most of it bad. The local TV station says the peace talks were adjourned at 11:00 P.M. In middle of the night, the alarm went off, and then the planes came. The truth is that the bombing intensified. People were unsurprised and depressed. They know their leaders and the world too well to hope for an easy, painless solution. But then this morning, my old war adrenaline came back. I know I must cope with whatever is going to happen to us hostages here. I just don't want to be pathetic and ridiculous, that's all. I predicted 2 June, but it turned out I'm a false Cassandra.

### 8 June

Last night, air raids again, low planes, bombs, fear, anger. But it's different from before, now we have peace problems, as well, the fear that the so-called peace will never be peaceful. We sat on the terrace and dealt with the consequences of peace. We probably won't have money, jobs, schools and democracy. No free space whatsoever. My father said, "Don't worry, we will build everything anew, democracy will come slowly, so don't go, but stay and help me in my old age." I don't believe him anymore. I know what he has needed me for all these years, to keep me down, to serve his wars and his ideas…That is my victory, his defeat, and my courage—to say no, to drink and to smoke in front of him, and, most of all, not to die for him.

## NATO and Serb military leaders sign a peace agreement.

### 9 June

In a way, this has been the worst year of my life. Looking in the mirror, I don't seem much older, a year or more doesn't make much difference in a middle-aged person. But looking around me, I notice a big difference. This can't be my life, my country, my friends, my relatives. It's painful and just hard to grow centuries in one year under such internal and external pressure. I made it, like most of the people around me. We all made it, holding hands or weapons, except for some who didn't, whose names we don't yet know. I am no longer a political idiot. I know I can't hide behind that mask anymore.

## 10 June

This is something new, a third phase of this war. After the invisible war, we had the aggressive war, and now I guess we'll have an everyday war. I went to the market to buy cherries, some salad, and a bottle of whiskey in celebration of a full night's sleep. The smugglers were jumping and clearing their tables in a panic. When I asked what was going on, somebody said: "It's an inspection, you crazy woman, how can you ask me such stupid questions?"

So I turned to a policeman, and said "Leave these people alone"—the political idiot speaking again. "They gave us food during all these terrible days."

He said very tolerantly, "Yes, but now we have peace. Off you go, before you get arrested for buying smuggled goods."

So this is peace, legality, and democracy—my new normality?


## 11 June

The political construct around me is rising from a ghost to a skeleton of New Order. Everybody won the war and wants to win even more. Will the sky we conquered with ceased bombings vanish into thin air: life without sky? Total political and private repression?

(The political ghost is rising. Everybody won the war.) I saw the Serbs from Kosovo in despair yesterday on BBC. They are now afraid to wait for NATO and get what they deserve, or not, from their former Albanian neighbors. I know that look on their faces, it's the same old conflict, going on and on. Then I met a Serb from Belgrade whose family is in Kosovo. He said his family and friends down there are begging him to find them a way out.

A young friend of mine who worked with refugees after her husband was mobilized, is in the hospital with a nervous breakdown. She can't walk. A doctor who protested against mobilization has been arrested as a traitor.

## The first NATO troops enter Kosovo as Serbian troops begin to leave.

### 12 June

War is slowly dropping out of our daily lives. Last night the bars and restaurants in my neighborhood reopened and the streets were full of people. The tension has gone, more lights are on, and shops once again sell Coca-Cola twenty-four hours a day. Today, troops are entering my country—people don't feel occupied, but they feel uneasy, just as they did in the first days of bombing. Nobody really knows what it means for the future. The only way to stay calm is to take it as it comes, and to use what we know from our history. But with Russians coming from the north, British from the south, soldiers of every color, like a Hollywood film, personally, I feel fine. I feel less isolated. Let them all come, let our histories mix—anything, as long as they don't build a wall.

**Jasmina Tesanovic** is a writer, editor, translator, publisher, teacher and filmmaker. Her writing in English has been published in *Granta* and the *Guardian* (U.K.). She is co-editor of *The Suitcase: Refugee Voices from Bosnia and Croatia.* She has translated many authors into Serbian, including Pier Paolo Pasolini, Elsa Morante, Italo Calvino, Joseph Brodsky, Hannah Arendt, Aldo Busi, and Karen Blixen. She is one of the founders of 94, the first feminist publishing house in Serbia. Her latest film, based on *The Diary of a Political Idiot* was presented at the 56th International Venice Film Festival in September 1999 and has been screened at numerous other festivals. Jasmina Tesanovic lives and works in Belgrade with her husband and children.

Journalist **Tim Judah** has covered the wars of the former Yugoslavia from the beginning. From 1991 to 1995 he was based in Belgrade as correspondent for the *Times* of London and the *Economist*. During that period, which covered the wars in Croatia and Bosnia, he witnessed the sieges of Vukovar, Dubrovnik and Sarajevo. He returned to London in 1995, but continued to cover Balkan affairs. In 1997 he published *The Serbs: History, Myth and the Destruction of Yugoslavia*. He covered the whole war in Kosovo for several British and US publications, including the New York Review of Books. In 1999 he published the first major account of the war, *Kosovo: War and Revenge*. He lives in London with his wife and five children.

## About Midnight Editions

MIDNIGHT EDITIONS is a new publishing venture whose mission is to enlarge our understanding of human rights by publishing works from regions where repression and censorship are currently endangering creative expression. We publish and promote the work of journalists, creative writers and photographers, engaged in the complex art of reporting and documenting history.

We welcome your comments. Please contact us:
www.midnighteditions.com
Email: fdelacoste@cleispress.com

*Selected books from Midnight Editions*

The Diary of a Political Idiot: Normal Life in Belgrade
by Jasmina Tesanovic
ISBN: 1-57344-114-7

No Place Like Home: Echoes from Kosovo
by Melanie Friend
ISBN: 1-57344-119-8

The Little School: Tales of Disappearance and Survival
By Alicia Partnoy
ISBN: 1-57344-029-9